MW00873805

WHAT CAN I DO?

What can I do?

CLYDE L. STRICKLAND

SALLIE W. BOYLES

What can I do?

For more information, contact www.WhatCanIDoBook.com.

For more information contact www.KathyFincher.com.

ISBN: 1979562954
ISBN 13: 9781979562959

I have endeavored to recreate events, locales and conversations from my memories of them and to share factual historic information. – Clyde L. Strickland

Clyde and Sandra Strickland at the dedication
of the Strickland Heart Center in Lawrenceville, Georgia.

This book is dedicated to
my Lord, Jesus Christ and God Almighty,
Who has protected me for seventy-eight years.

Thank you, Lord, for giving me my beautiful wife and angel Sandra,
who has reflected the example of Jesus every day for fifty-five years.

I also dedicate this book to Sandra and our three children,
Theresa, Michael and Kenneth,
who are committed to God, family, work, and America.

About My Dad, Clyde Strickland

I am Mike Strickland, devoted father of my only child Bailey, loving husband to my soulmate Haley, and proud middle son of Clyde and Sandra Strickland. I currently share the responsibility of running Metro Waterproofing, Inc., the business my dad founded, with my brother Kenneth, sister Theresa, and brother-in-law Skooter. I am the product of the years of encouragement, discipline and advice wielded by my parents throughout my childhood. Every kind or stern word molded me into the man I am today. Most importantly, I am the recipient of unconditional love—love shown through action, not mere words.

Ever since I can remember, I have told Dad that he should tell his story. So what does my dad do? What he always does: he acts and gets it done.

What Can I Do? is a product of the great American promise. It's the hope that all Americans, no matter your circumstances, can achieve anything you dream when you follow simple principles. It helps to have the heart of a lion and the drive of a freight train, like my dad.

When I meet people, especially in business, I tell them—with my chest out—that my dad is the all-American story: from leaving school in ninth grade to work on the farm, to becoming a successful entrepreneur. The stories of walking miles to school both ways in worn-out shoes are true. He had the advantages of food, shelter and family, but his home life was not the best. Many starting out with far better opportunities never advance. Dad's independent will is what set him free at age sixteen on the adventure that would be his life and legacy.

He is a proud veteran who appreciates the U.S. Army for the amazing, positive effect it made in his life. The military helped him catch up on missed education and let him see the world outside his small farming community of rural North Carolina. Obviously, the experience strengthened his patriotic love for this country. I have never met a person who loved America like Dad. Readers, I believe you will appreciate the way his patriotism shines through the words in this book.

You'll also gain life-changing knowledge from reading *What Can I Do?*—whether it's the inspiration of digging out of the trenches and climbing to the top of the corporate ladder, or the step-by-step advice my dad offers. (Much of what he imparts are one-liners that we call *Clyde-isms.*) I have learned through my dad and my other coaches and mentors that it takes only one or two positive thoughts to evoke major change in your life. That's the value of reading this book. Something will stick, whether you are a seven-year-old kid or a CEO of a Fortune 500 company.

I believe my dad's success is due to his basic, unbreakable principles by which he lives his life. They are simple, really, but many of us, for some reason, can't seem to put them all together: the love of God first; commitment to family; unbreakable morals and principles; treatment of all people with respect.

I am still amazed at how he can come down to the office, after being retired now for seventeen years, and talk with the lowest laborers in the company and treat them like they are friends and equals. I watch as their eyes light up, and they feel appreciated and motivated by his positive attitude. It's truly something to see. He has this effect on people of all ages.

When I try to explain the kind of man Dad is, I always tell this story: Most of us get on an elevator with a group of people and just stare at the floor. Dad gets on an elevator with ten people, and when the doors open, he knows all ten by name. He talks to everyone he walks by with a cheerful "Good morning!" and "How are you today?" So many of his greetings turn into real conversations and relationships.

Through his example, I have learned that you have to break out of your shell and speak up. If you don't, you miss out on life's greatest treasures. The person could be your future wife, a best friend, or the best client (Dad calls such people *friends*) in your business. When you love your job, you deal with friends, not clients. That philosophy sure has helped me in my career, and I am constantly working to improve on what Dad calls "getting to know your neighbors." It works and sure makes for a more fulfilled life.

I learned the concept of *mind over matter* from an early age. Heck, we all did. It meant that Dad had a secret cure for just about any problem. He knew that a strong mind could help overcome any obstacle. During my youth, when I wouldn't feel well in the morning, he'd say, "Take a shower; you will feel better." May sound crazy, but I did feel better and rarely missed school or work for the next forty years.

Dad's strong will comes from a strong, positive mind. Positive thinking can overcome negativity every time. If you can dream something, set a goal, and work tirelessly, you can achieve anything you put your mind to. This book is about taking action. Clyde Strickland is a man of action. While others are talking about doing something, Dad is getting it done.

No lack of education can stop a person who has drive and determination, although success has a different definition for us all. *What Can I Do?* will excite and inspire you to look inward to find the best version of you. You will realize that no matter your age or background, you are never down and out.

You will see how looking forward with a positive attitude will help you achieve your success.

I want to thank you, Dad, for always having the courage to stand out in the crowd, while knowing that it sometimes comes with ridicule and contempt; not being afraid to put it all on the line for what you believe in; showing me what a true leader looks like. Your strength, love, wisdom and faith have been a road map for my life. I know that readers of your book will draw inspiration from your life experiences as have the thousands you have already touched.

Dad, you are what I call a difference-maker. As your black sheep, I'm beyond blessed to have you as my wonderful, loving shepherd.

Love you, Dad.

Steven Michael Strickland
Son of Clyde Strickland
Vice President/Principal
Metro Waterproofing, Inc.

Acknowledgments

I would like to thank my wife, Sandra, for her love, dedication and hard work. She has made life a joy and made it possible for me to write this book. For fifty-five years, she has always been encouraging and has stood right beside me in every adventure I have taken on.

Thank God for my children, Theresa, Michael, and Kenneth, and my son Skooter (son-in-law) for their hard work and thoughtfulness that has given me time to write this book and to do all the things that God has called me to do in the last seventeen years, when I published *What Can I Do?* in its original version.

To my co-writer and editor, Sallie Boyles, who has used her penmanship, thoughts, and prayers to wade through all these dreams and miracles and put them in a form that people can understand.

To my adoptive son, Nathan McGill, one of the directors of the *American Made Movie*, for his organization and other skills for putting the final touches on the book.

To my long-time friend, Kathy Fincher, who designed the cover and helped with other parts of the book.

May God Bless everyone who reads this book and may God take them on a walk as wonderful as mine has been for the last seventy-eight years.

Introduction

What can I do?

Many ask the question with a feeling of helplessness: *How in the world could I possibly achieve anything great?*

Others believe that they have talents and choices, but need direction: *How can I use my abilities to succeed and make a difference?*

Some recognize that now is not the time to daydream, but to act: *Let's roll!*

"Are you ready? Okay. Let's roll."

Those were Todd Beamer's final words on September 11, 2001. He and several other passengers on United Airlines Flight 93 had joined forces to prevent four hijackers from turning their aircraft into a weapon of mass destruction. During an episode of calm, some had connected with their loved ones by phone. Todd ended up having a heartfelt conversation with Lisa Jefferson, a supervisor and operator with GTE, one of the cellular providers. From what the people on the ground told them, the American heroes well understood that the United States was under siege by terrorists. In the worst attack, ever, on this country's soil, two separate commercial planes had already plowed into the World Trade Center towers in New York City, and another had crashed into the Pentagon in Washington, D.C.

Hoping and praying their fate would be different, the passengers could have sat quietly, as warned by the hijackers. The Islamic jihadists had already slit the throats of the captain and copilot. Instead, Todd and his gang of strong-willed cabin mates fought back. Mustering all their might and courage, they stormed the cockpit. Tragically, the aircraft crashed nose first into a field in Shanksville, Pennsylvania. All aboard perished. Even so, the valiant move saved an untold number of other innocent souls in Washington, D.C., the hijackers' destination, and spared the national treasure they meant to destroy.

It's still hard for me to realize that I had taken Sandra on her first trip to New York City in November of 2000 and we went to the top of the World Trade Center. We'll never forget looking over city. I also remember seeing the heavy security and mentioning to Sandra that no one with an idea of causing trouble could get into that building.

Evil forces don't easily give up, but good souls never quit.

Taking every death and bit of destruction personally, we Americans came together after 9-11. Patriotism seemed stronger than ever before. Looking back over America's history, we find other examples of the greatest optimism, along with faith and courage, during our darkest, most challenging times.

We are living in such times right now, although some groups and certain individuals with various political ideas and motives have no desire to unify. They're fueling division among citizens as a weapon against the United States of America.

Make no mistake about it: Our country remains under attack—from within. Politically correct politicians and media are leading the orchestrated assault on our way of life. Filling our minds with downright lies, they're tricking us to give up our Constitutional and God-given rights, particularly the freedom to worship our Lord God Almighty. They are enemies of the values that once made America the envy of all other nations.

While America still claims to be "the land of opportunity" as "one Nation under God," we need everyday heroes to step up and unleash the spirit that built this country. That means each one of us must identify what we can do—for God, self, family, community and country—and then get busy. Some recognize what they are called to do from the start. Others take longer, but we should all keep our eyes open to opportunities and commit to leading a purposeful life each day.

Proving that the possibilities are endless, *What Can I Do?* shares my personal stories—the ones that shaped who I am—and my most priceless, hard-earned insights. May they inspire and guide your endeavors.

Clyde Strickland

Table of Contents

Big, Black Cadillac

Lawrenceville, Georgia, the second oldest city in the metro Atlanta area and my home for many years now, used to be a small town. Our region boomed in the 1980s, when Gwinnett County became the fastest growing county in the entire country. Before that happened, taking a quick errand to our little downtown guaranteed we'd encounter several friends on the sidewalks and in stores. From stopping multiple times to chat each time we went out, no one planned to finish a shopping trip quickly, and that was just fine. My family and I cherished the warm, comforting feeling of knowing every person and at least one identifying characteristic about each adult and child.

The one thing that all seemed to know about me was that I bought a brand-new Lincoln Continental each year. As a practical matter, I had to replace my automobiles annually from driving them like trucks across muddy, bumpy construction sites and wearing out the suspension. I could have chosen another type of car, and those who didn't know me probably thought I was showing off with the Continental. In truth, I wanted to show my respect for the people I dealt with in business and to receive the same from them.

Others in my line of work were known to arrive on jobsites looking rather scruffy. Most drove an old pickup. I presented myself so that customers and contractors would form a higher opinion of Metro Waterproofing from their first impression. When I not only rolled up in a shiny new Lincoln, but also dressed like a banker, they saw me as someone who was successful, capable and committed.

More importantly to me, a shining, glittering luxury car represented a profound symbol of self-reliance and independence.

In sharp contrast, I grew up on a sharecropper's spread where, to me, nothing shined. Despite the endless rows of bright green tobacco plants, the property's trees, and other natural elements, in my mind, I see the farm in shades of brown, tea-stained like a photograph taken by an old-fashioned camera. The pictures from my memories focus on the dull, brown earth that we farmed. The original colors of our house, its contents, and our clothes may have been bright one day, too, but they were plain and drab for as long as I could recall, and so were our lives.

Farm life demanded that my family and I sacrificed any secret ambition; we existed to work for our survival. Those rare moments of individual gratification—a hit in a baseball game; a date with a pretty girl—were fleeting, teasing releases from the routine of continuous chores and identical days. Granted, the farm taught us the value of hard work and family loyalty, but it offered no anticipation of escaping, no outlet to fulfill our fundamental human need for independence.

Looking around me, I saw no glimmer of hope. Our neighbors and farmhands were similarly trapped in the struggle. The only diamond among us, Mr. Jordan, owned the farm we rented. The tailored suits he wore at church inspired awe in contrast to the farmers' washed-out denims and khakis. His genteel manners seemed perfectly regal compared to our hillbilly simplicity. Moreover, in the eyes of a farm boy who had never set foot outside rural Johnson County, North Carolina, nothing about Mr. Jordan surpassed the heavenly spectacle of his glittering black Cadillac as it glided along our dirt drive.

About every month, when Mr. Jordan dropped by to collect our rent, my father welcomed him with a ritual meant to honor his landlord by showing respect for him. The preparations began on the day before his visit with my brothers and me going to the riverbanks to cut choice hickory kindling. By the time that we'd dragged the branches back home to the barbecue pit, my father would have slaughtered and bled our fattest hog. Using the sweet hickory, he would begin slow-cooking the pork at sundown for the next day's lunch. Along with preparing succulent, fall-off-the-bone barbecue, he'd retrieve a jug of his purest corn whiskey from the cotton fields, where it had been well hidden from revenuers (those pesky U.S. Treasury Department agents in charge of enforcing laws against bootlegging alcoholic beverages).

Worn out from a late night of tending to the hickory pit, we boys could only stare as that magical Cadillac, its tail-fins polished to a sheen, rolled into the front yard. Getting a whiff of the man's scent—talcum and cologne—as Jordan himself finally emerged from the car, turned us into dumb-struck statues with our mouths hanging open. Dirty, hungry and envious, we children had no choice but to watch from a respectable distance, while the men gorged on the barbecue ribs, the best cut of meat, and sipped the powerful moon-shine. Waiting for eternity, until they couldn't muster another bite, we picked what was left on the few bones that remained.

Above all, what Mr. Jordan and his riches (his mammoth car and fine clothes) most represented to me was independence. While we labored for survival and placed the family before any of our individual needs, Mr. Jordan came and went as he pleased. Obviously, he enjoyed the life he had earned for himself and the respect he received from others.

During one of his visits, I made a solemn vow to myself, and I remained devoted to that vow for most of the next twenty years of my life: one day, Clyde Strickland would be behind the wheel of his *own* big, black Cadillac.

The farm, with all its simple virtues, enslaved us, and the big car seemed like the only way out of the fields. In my mind, it represented a life of personal freedom, one that would allow me to satisfy my burning hunger—not for comfort, but for independence. I wanted to learn at school in the way that the town kids were educated. I wanted to see the world that I'd glimpsed at The Bijou (our town's movie theater). I wanted to raise a family who'd never suffer the hardships of my boyhood. I wanted to face a sunrise that signaled something more than a workday so grueling that it would drain any man or woman's humanity.

My sisters had told me I'd been born with a "sweet spirit," so more than anything, when I dreamed about my life, I wanted the opportunity to express myself by loving and helping others.

At the age of thirty-six, I bought my first Cadillac, a beautiful 1973 coupe. Having flashbacks of Mr. Jordan's visits and the decades of work and determination that had earned me that symbol of independence, I took possession of my car with a rush of pride and pleasure. I was giggling like a boy and continued to grin and chuckle when, only four blocks from the dealership, I felt and heard a strange rumble from the engine. As the sound got louder, smoke bellowed from beneath the hood. With no other options, I rolled my symbol of independence to the shoulder of the road. The transmission had given out, and I was stranded on Church Street in the heart of Decatur, Georgia.

Today, if that would happen in the same location (it's about seven miles from downtown Atlanta), I'd pray no one would hit my car or run over me. Back then, I would have been lucky if any vehicle passed. I was all alone and trudging up the street because my brand-new car was a broken-down lemon. Instead of turning red and losing my temper,

I couldn't stop beaming like an idiot. Looking back at the smoking vehicle and smiling so widely that my cheeks hurt, I whispered to no one, but myself, "That's my Cadillac!"

As a matter of preference, I switched to Lincolns in 1975, when I bought my first Continental. No doubt, the gossipers in town had plenty to say, but that never mattered to me. My luxury cars have always embodied the commitment I made long ago: to foster my independence and likewise share the benefits of my freedom and prosperity with my family and community.

When in the driver's seat, I remember the burning hunger in the belly of a dirty farm boy who'd vowed to escape the drudgery of the poverty to which he'd been born. Recalling that child keeps me aware of the fact that my good fortune is meaningless unless I strive with all my might to bestow it upon others.

Boom!

Before the age of sophisticated equipment and chemicals, farmers had dynamite and mules to clear their land. My father might have been unschooled and illiterate, but he was an expert in using explosives to demolish any stump or root that got in his way. On one occasion, I remember how we boys, not even ten years old, observed him as he gingerly stepped around a stubborn old tree stump to position the caps of dynamite. Then, from a safe distance away, we picked up an impressionable lesson in how to send chunks of wood and globs of dirt shooting high into the sky.

Explosions notwithstanding, my dull, hard childhood didn't provide much fun or excitement, yet I found an escape in the war and cowboy movies (we called them "pictures") featured at the local theater every weekend. On our rare afternoons of leisure, my brothers and I loved to star in our own adventures as those big-screen heroes, and we fought many pretend battles with brooms for rifles and clods of dirt for grenades. After spying on our father and picking up tips on how to play with dynamite, we decided to make ourselves a real explosion.

Huddled in our makeshift war room behind the tobacco barn, my brother Doug and I discussed the details of the mission. Ecstatic over our clever decision to make Halloween Eve the time for demolition, we miraculously managed to keep our plan a secret. On the chosen hour, we met in the cotton field with three tobacco sticks (long wooden poles used to cure tobacco), which would support the fuses, and three sticks of dynamite. Our father had rarely used more than one dynamite stick at a time, but Doug and I wanted our bomb to make a lasting impression.

We covertly planted the explosive sticks among the harvest-ready cotton and synchronized our Hopalong Cassidy (the fictional cowboy hero of the day) watches. The only task left was to light the fuses. They were long enough to allow us to sprint to the movie theater, one mile away, and escape suspicion.

Just as we reached the ticket window, a flash of fire lit the distant sky and a boom traveled across the fields towards town. Mission accomplished! At last, we'd produced a nighttime adventure in rural North Carolina that was far more thrilling than any of the heroic exploits Hollywood could have staged for our amusement! Equally as important, we'd brought some excitement to the dismal lives of farmers, who had to be wondering about the cause of the calamity that had jarred them from their evening rest.

We had no idea how much excitement we'd stirred up until reaching our driveway and seeing our father amid an irate mob of neighbors. He was assuring them that he'd repair any damages they'd sustained; thankfully, recognizing that my father's word was better than a legal guarantee bearing some official stamp, they settled into a grumble and wandered back to their respective homes. That's when our father led Doug and me to our punishment.

After administering the most unforgettable whipping of a lifetime, our father recounted our Halloween mission's casualties, which had exceeded our intended target by a considerable measure. The explosion's force had blown out the panes of every single window that faced the field within a 300-yard radius. Even worse, the bomb had virtually destroyed my father's valuable cotton crop, just ready for harvest. Instead of the rows of plants that were expected to yield about one bale (495 pounds) of cotton, my father had one ugly strip of barren land—thirty feet wide by one hundred feet long.

Could we ever undo the damage? Ashamed and grief-stricken, we didn't believe so.

In the end, we learned two indelible lessons: First, never guess how much dynamite you'll need for an explosion; be *absolutely* precise in your calculations. Second, mistakes are soon forgotten when you accept responsibility for them.

The whole harvest long, Doug and I labored—in the dark hours—before and after our already backbreaking day. Our mindset was to earn enough money to replace our neighbors' shattered window panes before the winter's cold reached North Carolina. In that effort, we harvested their crops, trapped and sold wild rabbits, and left off our weekly trip to the movies until our father agreed, without saying a word, that our debt had been repaid.

By acknowledging our fault and working to correct our mistake, we earned our victims' forgiveness. To our surprise, we also earned their respect. They were accustomed to the pranks of mischievous boys, but we shocked and touched them through our earnest attempts to make amends for the havoc we'd caused.

Thinking back, I am forever grateful for my father, who did not let us off with a mild scolding. He did not repair the damage his children produced. He also didn't beat us while preaching that we would never be worthwhile human beings. Instead, he taught us to accept responsibility for our actions, to clean up the mess on our own, and to experience forgiveness.

Since that incident, no dilemma in my life has ever seemed so overwhelming to me that I could not resolve it. For that reason, many have called me overconfident, and countless times I have proven them right by failing. However, I have never sat idly by and watched a mess spread. I have never waited for some magic janitor to materialize and mop up any casualty on my behalf.

Thanks to my father's response to our Halloween-prank-gone-wrong-at-harvest-time, I have always believed that I could clean up any problem. Whether I generated the mess myself or someone else made it for me, my reaction has been to search for a solution and get to work.

Looking, Listening and Learning

With a softly rounded face and sweet smile that reminded me of an angel, Mrs. Boyd taught eighth grade at Wilson's Mills School. The year was 1952, and she was the first and only schoolteacher in my life who didn't presume a farm boy had nothing to contribute to her class.

In Wilson's Mills, as in most small, Southern, farming communities, the citizens—farm owners, merchants who served the farm owners, and farm workers—coexisted, but they represented three distinct social classes. The children of owners and merchants appeared at school each day dressed in clean, crisply pressed clothes that their mothers had purchased brand new from Hudson Belk, the local department store. Arriving promptly on time with their homework completed, unless they were sick, boys and girls from the upper and middle classes sat confidently in the front rows.

The kids of sharecroppers, wearing worn-out overalls and brogans (leather ankle boots), showed up only when the crops and their related chores allowed. On the rare times that they spent a full day in class, the part-time students sat silently in the back, pre-warned by their teachers not to interfere with the regular children's education. Barely able to read, physically exhausted and discouraged, the disadvantaged kids inevitably trailed behind the other boys and girls in their studies.

I missed more school than I attended. Chopping cotton or pulling corn all day was my usual excuse, but on one occasion, I was absent after a cow had gored my nose. The wound was so broad that when I tried to stop the bleeding with my hand, my finger went all the way through the side of my nostril. Today, anyone, no matter how poor, can receive treatment in an emergency room. Back then, if we had no money for the doctor, we settled for a home remedy. My mother sewed my gaping wound shut with the same needle and thread that she used to mend our clothes!

From those of us who spent most of our time working and enduring life's hardships, an education seemed a luxury. Fortunately, I was blessed with a good memory and quick intellect, so I managed to pass every grade, but not without humiliation. Along with the teachers' telling every boy like me to keep quiet, as if we were burdens they had to tolerate, the well-dressed, well-spoken kids from town ridiculed our country accents and ragged attire.

Mrs. Boyd was the exception. She possessed the wisdom and compassion to recognize that despite our callused hands and sunburned faces, we deserved her attention like any other child in her class. In fact, she granted us more of her time and focus because our need was greater. Sensing my eagerness to learn, she one day made an unprecedented decision in asking me to move to the front row.

That was the same year Hurricane Hazel swept through North Carolina. Toppling trees and blowing cars across parking lots throughout the state, the storm raged as far inland as Johnston County, sixty miles from the coast. The fallen trees on Mr. Jordan's farm landed in such thick piles that we had to clear our way into our house with a crosscut saw and axes.

Considering the effects of Hurricane Hazel and the attitude of Mrs. Boyd, I acquired a valuable lesson in 1952. Hazel had shown that the material possessions which separated me from the other children were as flimsy as pine trees—towering above us today, they could be broken sticks on the ground tomorrow. Right before the storm hit, Johnson County enjoyed one of its finest days; with the sun striking the morning dew, the corn and tobacco glittered in the fields like jewels. On the day after Hazel raged, huge tracts of fertile North Carolina soil looked like they'd been trampled and bulldozed. From the richest to the poorest, families lost everything—almost. Thanks to Mrs. Boyd, I observed that no outside force could destroy one special kind of wealth: an individual's education.

The School of Life

The farm eventually forced me to abandon my formal schooling altogether. By the time I turned sixteen, my older brothers had moved away, so my father had only Doug and me to tend the crops each day. Nevertheless, thanks to Mrs. Boyd's encouragement and her faith in my talent, I knew that no matter how many days of school I missed or the hardships I faced, my learning would continue and the fruits of my education, in whatever form it came, would last my entire life.

I made up my mind to learn everything I could, although it was a ragged quilt of an education, stitched together from whatever information came my way. At sixteen, I had barely set foot outside Johnston County. The annual visit to my married sisters' homes, just thirty miles away, felt like an ocean voyage. Although confined to such a small area beyond the farm, I realized I could learn plenty by observing the world around me.

In the mornings, I watched the wrens fight the wind and rain to build their nests, twig by twig. In the evenings, I watched the beavers slowly haul branches to the mammoth dam that had taken them almost three years to complete and the rest of their lives to maintain. When they finished the barrier, I could see how they had permanently changed the course of the stream. When I went rabbit hunting with my dog, I noticed that a good dog never gave up on the chase. He would track that rabbit forever—until I killed the game or he caught it.

Studying the animals' patience and persistence would reward me later when I started my own waterproofing business with one battered pickup truck and a pledge to myself to be the top company servicing the largest city in the South. A friend had laughed at my audacity to christen my one-truck company with such a big name as *Metro.* He couldn't see my vision to serve the entire metropolitan area. Thanks to the birds that didn't let bad weather keep them from finishing their nests, the beavers that spent three years swimming upstream with construction materials, and the dogs that never gave up on the hunt, I knew that patience and persistence would win the day. (Guided by my ambitious vision, our family business today provides service well beyond Metro Atlanta!)

Working the farm carried its own lessons. On a sharecropper's spread, necessity was the mother of invention. In other words, poverty forced us to squeeze every ounce left from the scant resources available to us. Mules and men worked from sunrise to sunset, often with tools comprised of more rust than metal. Old clothes passed from brother to brother until they were rags. The tattered cloth was then cut into patches and sewn into quilts. Everything and everyone had a use; you just had to possess the ingenuity to figure out what the purpose was. I never forgot that concept, one that has served me from the time that Metro Waterproofing was just getting off the ground.

A Wino's Lesson

Patience and persistence wins the day—always. Likewise, any source can qualify as a teacher. An old wino reminded me of that many years later, when I owned Metro Waterproofing. By that time, we had grown and were handling jobs outside Georgia, but I was still performing manual labor alongside my crews. On that day, we were working on the Federal Building in Jacksonville, Florida.

Dressed in a dingy coat, the man wandered towards us and looked on for a bit as we painstakingly removed old caulking with carpet knives. The task was one of the most tedious and time-consuming steps in preparing to apply new waterproofing. "If I was cutting that caulk out," the man volunteered, slurring his words, "I'd use a jigsaw." (He was referring to a knife with a narrow, jagged blade.) With that, he staggered on down the street.

Confident that he knew better, the foremen on the job ignored the fellow, but my farming background had taught me to be resourceful. If presented a seemingly logical idea for accomplishing a job with less work, I was then willing to give it a try. In no time, I was driving to the nearest Sears, where I bought the most durable jigsaw knife and blade they sold. I then got to work on the caulk removal.

Amazingly, with that saw, I removed the dried caulking far more quickly and easily than the other four workers in total could using the old method. Oh, you can rest assured that we all switched to jigsaws, and by the end of that job, Metro Waterproofing had not only depleted the entire stock in Jacksonville's stores, but Black and Decker, the maker of the knife, was also shipping cases of them directly to us at the Federal Building. That's not the end of the story. Today, jigsaws are standard equipment in our industry. Toolmakers now manufacture that type of blade with the sole purpose of removing caulk. Incredibly, the unique line of tools exists because a pitiful old wino recognized a better way to get a job done and a North Carolina plowboy had the sense to listen to him.

Ingenuity and success come from listening, observing, and trial and error. When young, bright college-educated employees first join our company, they love to ask us what we want them to do. My own children have each asked that question. My answer always is to tell them to go out and make mistakes—not recklessly, of course, but by testing reasonable options, learning, and adjusting. We also encourage them to let their hearts and minds guide them to do what is right. Their growth results from acknowledging what went wrong, evaluating the reasons why, and not repeating the mistake.

Still a Schoolboy and a Teacher

Knowledge is everywhere—beneath a haggard face or within a rusted tool. Often, the lessons imparted in everyday yet unexpected ways impact us more profoundly that those culled from formal training. Perhaps that's why two North American writers, Grant Allen (1848-1899) and Mark Twain (1835-1910), are so often quoted: "I have never let my schooling interfere with my education."

My intent is not to imply that traditional education lacks value. When I joined the Army as a half-educated, high school dropout, I immediately noted the advantages that other soldiers had over me. They knew so much more of the world and quickly grasped the vast amounts of technical knowledge that the Army introduced to us. I had to work twice as hard to keep abreast of the training. To close the gap, I set myself to studying every piece of written information that came my way.

Beginning with Western adventures and crime novels, I devoured Mickey Spillane's easy-to-read suspense stories that I purchased from the dime stores that sold items for no more than ten cents. When my reading level progressed, I expanded my choices. A necessity and a joy, my habit of reading continues to this day; in fact, I possibly read as much (and on the same level) as the average college professor. My college-educated children tell me that I read considerably more than they do, and for pure entertainment, I prefer a book to the blare of a television.

Whatever the source of my learning, I believe that I've acquired more knowledge of the world *because of* my life on the farm. Aside from Mrs. Boyd, the beloved teacher who encouraged me in her class, most of my experiences in school were limiting. Therefore, hungry for knowledge, I kept my eyes open for any situation that provided a lesson. Truly, much of what I've observed and absorbed would have escaped me if I'd relied on formal teachers and classrooms for my education.

Learning is all about keeping your eyes open like a child and looking around, as if seeing everything for the first time. Be curious. Ask questions and seek answers. Don't assume you've already been there and done that.

Independence Day and Lifelong Responsibility

One evening, after endless days of trucking tobacco from the hot, humid fields, my father and I stood at a wooden bench, where we graded the leaves, judging each by its quality that would dictate price. The brighter and fuller the leaf, the richer the crop. During that process, I pulled a leaf that had just a tinge of brown—so little that almost any grader would have scored it into the more valuable pile. I did just that. My father caught what he deemed was my mistake and wasted no time questioning my judgement.

Sixteen years old and confident of my ability to grade tobacco, I responded offhandedly that I saw no defect in the leaf I held. I was still gazing at the leaf when I felt the back of his callused hand smash against my jaw. The force sent me sprawling over the grading bench. Receiving that sort of brutality from Frank Strickland was nothing new, but after enduring his treatment my entire life, I could take no more. With as much courage as sixteen-year-old boy could muster,

I swore to him that if he ever hit me again, I would kill him. Then, marching out of the barn and straight to our house, I packed every item of my clothing in a small suitcase and set out down the country road. I never went home again.

Unlike other teenagers in 1956, who were busy going to sock hops and drive-in movies, I moved out of my parents' home and in with my brother's family near Greenville, North Carolina. For three solid weeks, my sister-in-law drove me around town to assist my search for a non-farming job—a tough order in the rural South back then. Finally, Wilbur Hardee, owner of the Silo, one of Greenville's busiest restaurants, agreed to interview me. His name probably sounds familiar: Mr. Hardee founded the fast-food chain, Hardee's.

To meet my potential boss, I followed a waitress with the thought that she was leading me into an office; instead, she took me into a steaming kitchen. Wearing a spotless white chef's hat and dressed immaculately, the man I aimed to impress immediately struck me as someone I could respect. Speaking up, I swore to him that from laboring on a farm since the day I could walk, I would prove myself to be his hardest worker. Apologetically, he replied that he didn't have a job for me.

Dejected, I returned to my brother's home. Having promised to mow his lawn that afternoon, I had just turned one row when I spotted a long, pink Lincoln as it rolled into the driveway. Wilbur Hardee was behind the wheel. Without stepping from the car, he leaned out the window and said, "After the way you talked, I expected to find you working somewhere. I decided to give you a job. Do you think you can learn to cook?"

I told him I was determined to learn anything necessary to make a wage. He informed me that for six days of labor, my pay would be thirty-five dollars per week plus two meals daily.

The next morning, I showed up prepared to prove myself, and for the first two days, Mr. Hardee put me to the test. From the time that I arrived, to the time I left the Silo, I peeled pound after pound of shrimp. My hands ached from the repetitive motion, but neither the monotony nor the discomfort caused me to complain. Peeling shrimp was a great deal easier than sweating down row after row of tobacco!

My First Promotion

During the first two weeks of my employment at the Silo, I walked, ran, and thumbed (hitchhiked) six miles to and from work each way. I had to leave home by three in the morning to be at work by five. Living in the country, we didn't have a rapid-transit system that would have enabled me to hop on a bus or subway.

Securing reliable transportation was my priority, so when I received my first paycheck after two weeks, I bought a car for $150. I intended to arrive on time every morning and stay as late as necessary each evening to keep that job and get promoted. I paid ten dollars down and made weekly payments of five dollars. After earning my raise, I increased my payments to own that vehicle outright as soon as possible.

Less than thrilled with me, possibly because I was a harder worker than he, the head cook began treating me badly. He assigned me the most awful kitchen jobs—peeling the potatoes and shrimp, washing dirty dishes, cleaning out the cooler—instead of putting my other talents to work. On top of that, while I performed those hard, dirty jobs, the cook cursed me with every word he uttered.

On one afternoon, after taking all I could tolerate, I retreated to the back of the restaurant to peel my potatoes in solitude. Mr. Hardee soon found me there and wanted to know why I'd left the kitchen. Quite bluntly, I let him know that I'd endured more than enough cruelty on the farm, and although I greatly appreciated the opportunity he'd given me, I refused to work for anyone who cursed me. Without hesitating, Mr. Hardee asked if I could handle the head cook's responsibilities. I said that I could do any job in the restaurant with the proper instruction.

On that same afternoon, Mr. Hardee fired the jealous cook and promoted me to fill his spot. Over the next few weeks, as my employer guided me through the steps, I knew for certain that the only formula for success involved a work ethic like my father had instilled. I also learned an invaluable lesson from Mr. Hardee: The boss must be personally committed. From the first day that I began training with him and through the next two years that I worked at Silo, I watched him demand the highest standards of quality—nothing less, no matter the cost—of himself.

My dedication to the job during the first two days after my promotion confirmed the confidence I'd expressed when interviewed. Mr. Hardee raised my salary to forty-five dollars per week. He also began teaching me the Silo's recipes and preparations. My first job off the farm was proving to me that no matter the occupation, a natural balance existed between the work and the yield.

Quality First

Believing he had found a means to raise his already superior benchmarks, Mr. Hardee purchased an expensive hamburger-making machine. Nothing more than a stainless-steel tractor belt and a broiler, the gadget advertised the ability to cook perfectly uniform beef patties and buns. Back in the 1950s, the automated piece of equipment seemed an utterly revolutionary tool, and Mr. Hardee was eager to deliver consistent quality without manual labor. The worker simply loaded the machine.

Before the week ended, we realized that the hamburger factory was far from perfect. Burgers exited the line in all stages—charred to raw—and every bun emerged as stiff as cardboard. Without a tinge of remorse, Mr. Hardee removed the state-of-the-art dud from the kitchen and chunked it in the alley behind the Silo. Long after I left the restaurant, the useless but shiny hunk of stainless steel remained there, glistening under the North Carolina sunshine and reminding me that many plans seems like bright ideas until they are put to the test!

Mr. Hardee continually worked to raise his high standards even higher, and if he attempted to achieve a goal with a new method or machine that failed, he admitted defeat and moved to another strategy. Like my father, he never sacrificed his work ethic for the sake of a dollar. Likewise, he was never idle. "If you're not working," Mr. Hardee would say, "you're wiping." In other words, some task could always be accomplished with a broom or a cloth! For that reason, his restaurants consistently received A ratings from the North Carolina Department of Standards. On one occasion, when the Silo received a high B, my employer closed the restaurant for the day. That move cost him hundreds of dollars—a fortune in those years—yet Mr. Hardee wouldn't reopen until the restaurant was reevaluated and earned the A.

Ethical Treatment of Employees

Thanks to Mr. Hardee's unshakable work ethic and superior standards, my fellow employees and I had jobs. Customers could count on the Silo for quality food and service, so they were loyal to the restaurant. Therefore, we felt morally compelled to honor the opportunity to work for him. Through Mr. Hardee, we further recognized the connection between responsibility and loyalty—both to one's employees and one's customers.

An employer's compassion for his workers is a matter of ethics. Mr. Hardee achieved utmost productivity from his employees by rewarding their contributions to the business and respecting their humanity. The pay, although modest, was fair, and his caring attitude made the long hours an easy burden.

My father, in contrast, understood that the soil rewarded him for his labor, yet he didn't grasp the need to reward his sons, even though we each worked as hard as our young bodies could abide. Consequently, he drove us away, one by one, and ended up alone to tend his farm.

In many cases, children who suffer the kind of savagery my brothers and I experienced end up inflicting the same torment on their own families, friends and employees. Thankfully, I've managed to control the temper my father beat into me. Aside from believing such violence was inexcusable, I recognized that others were inclined to help me if I had a kind and caring demeanor towards them.

Without question, an employer who exploits his employers ultimately compromises the integrity of the work ethic he instills to the same degree as the employee who abuses the privileges of the job.

My father didn't see that we boys would have given him the all-important extras that coincide with respect and love, if we hadn't been laboring out of fear. Mr. Hardee, in comparison, understood that his fairness and compassion earned such respect from his employees that we felt compelled to treat his restaurant as if it were our own. As a matter of fact, I once caught an older cook stealing ham. By confronting him, I took the risk of receiving whatever revenge he might have decided to inflict. When the man told me to mind my own business, I said, "Looking after my boss's property *is* my business." Just sixteen, I'd felt responsible and told Mr. Hardee. (The man never stole another ham.)

Treating my own employees with the same dignity and compassion became my first moral responsibility in business and a matter of maintaining my own work ethic. By creating an environment that inspired my employees of Metro Waterproofing to work hard—not because they had to, but because they wanted to—my business achieved a wonderful balance between my duty to them and their duty to a company that fully appreciated their commitment.

To this day, we all understand that by our maintaining a strong work ethic, Metro Waterproofing provides us a comfortable life and a good living. If we don't work, we don't eat!

The Right Person for the Job

A positive attitude among my employees also prevails because I've always made a point of placing them in jobs they loved to do. When they love the work, they are good at it. A happy worker is a great worker. Few of our employees leave us to work elsewhere unless they're doing something to better themselves, such as going into business for themselves.

We've hired many people to work at Metro Waterproofing who've spent an entire career with us, but in the mid-1980s, we were having a lot of turnover in our accounting office. We couldn't find the right person to fill the controller position. After I hired a guy named Fred and had to let him go, I got it in my mind to put a woman in that spot. I thought a female would have better skills and patience for all the paperwork. After interviewing three women, I decided on the one I wanted to hire and asked her to meet me the next day for a final interview.

Even though I had made up my mind, the agent from the recruiting firm I was using, Snelling and Snelling (today, the company name is Snelling), called to say she had the perfect person and I needed to interview *him*. I told her that I'd already made a decision. She insisted, saying, "You have to interview this guy." I flatly said, "I'm not interviewing no damn man!" I'd had enough of guys messing up in the job. She kept saying that he would be the perfect person, so just out of respect for her, I agreed to interview Sam.

From the moment Sam walked in, I could tell he was an old country boy. It was 1985, and he was wearing a 1950s' sports coat and a cowboy tie. As it turned out, Sam loved John Wayne.

The more we talked, the more I realized how much I liked him and how much we had in common. For one thing, Sam was raised in Selma, North Carolina, my hometown, but I didn't bother to tell Sandra that right away. She didn't think anything that came from Selma was good except for me, so I hired him and waited two weeks before revealing that one fact.

Sam turned out to be one of the greatest assets to Metro Waterproofing that we ever had. He was my right hand for thirty years. When I turned the company over to the kids and they began to expand their knowledge, they'd want to change procedures. Sam, however, was still the controller, and he'd make them follow the policy until he okayed the change with me. Sandra and I might be out of the country, but Sam would say he had to get "the man on the phone" first.

He retired at sixty-five, but now that he's in his late seventies, Sam still goes in the office. He trains new hires and checks on things. He's part of our family. He does woodworking as a hobby, so he'll drop by my house to collect birdhouses that need repair. Sam will rebuild the little structures at his place and then return them like new without even bothering to tell me.

That was God working through the Snelling agent in finding my right hand for Metro Waterproofing.

My advice is to put people where they'll be happy and then load the wagon; in other words, always give those who report to you more to accomplish than they think they can do. The job shouldn't greatly exceed a person's skills or knowledge, but rather each small task should use an individual's talents and present challenges that build confidence when accomplished.

People are also more satisfied when they remain busy. I've further found that certain employees, like those in management training, benefit from having so much to do they must take some of their work home to finish. From my experience, they end up becoming super workers by striving to achieve more. If the challenge is too small, they'll tend to drag out the task.

An Opportunity on Every Corner

Chores on my father's farm, various jobs as a teenager, and the Army all provided me stable, risk-free opportunities to support myself. From my earliest days on the farm, I had learned that every worker must fully contribute his or her labor to an enterprise so that it would succeed. When looking down on my plate and seeing the peas, corn and meat that I'd helped to raise and harvest, I knew that there was no such thing as a free lunch.

While I made myself useful in every role, my early jobs required nothing more from me than my hard labor and commitment. Someone else always shouldered the responsibility of making the crucial decisions that determined the fate of the venture. My father was the one who figured out how much cotton we would plant. Mr. Hardee and my other employers set the price of their products and services. Uncle Sam (the cartoon character created to personify the U.S. Government) assigned my fellow soldiers and me to the places and positions that best suited the mission.

Granted, allowing the people in power to call the shots has its advantages. If you perform your simple job, those in control reward you with a comfortable existence, free of the concerns and stress that come with being in charge. What you give up is control of your destiny. The same applies to giving up personal freedoms by letting your government have too much say and control over what's best for you and your fellow citizens.

Knowing that a trustworthy authority is looking out for them, younger children in a family, lower-level employees, or soldiers might rest easily at night. I never felt that sense of peace. Although I thoroughly respected the men for whom I worked and served, as well as their teachings, I realized that their power kept me from attaining independence. As a young man, however, I also recognized that I needed to have patience until I acquired the survival skills and practical knowledge necessary to take full responsibility for my life. Among them, I was blessed with the perfect teacher, my father-in-law.

Pops

Clinton Edward Catlett, Sandra's father, was a self-made man who determined his own fortunes and failures. A master carpenter, he was a wizard with a hammer and nail. While I picked up some great tips about craftsmanship, the examples he set as an entrepreneur taught me most of what I know about business.

Aside from fate, my father's ignorance and fear had kept him chained to the land as a sharecropper. In contrast, Mr.

Catlett, or *Pops* to his children and me, was innovative, adaptable and unafraid to take risks. Blessed with a gift of calculating the dollars and cents to run successful businesses, he owned an ice cream store, a doughnut shop, a fish market, and a grocery store at various times in life. Of all his talents, Pops's real passion was produce. He loved surveying the farmers' markets to find the best deals. He then meticulously scheduled his fruit and vegetable deliveries to arrive at their freshest, so customers welcomed the quality goods he provided at a reasonable price.

When I went to work for Pops, my goal was to learn as much as possible as his business partner. The laws of supply and demand, which explain how prices rise and fall based on a product's perceived value and availability, was lesson one. Likewise, I quickly understood that the tasks and costs related to ensuring higher quality often meant netting lower profits in the short term; in the long term, we'd earn more money by developing satisfied customers who remained loyal to us. Pops further taught me to understand how to satisfy our customers: to read them by listening and observing, and supply what they needed without ever deceiving them. The point was to treat people kindly and fairly, just as I'd want to be treated, putting them first and doing what was right. If we made our customers happy, then we'd stay in business.

As an entrepreneur, Pops was my role model, but not because vending produce was an innovative idea. Aside from being one of the world's oldest businesses, the operating procedures for selling fruits and vegetables were rather basic. Such work, however, allowed Clinton Edward Catlett to answer to himself, and the freedom and responsibility appealed to him. His profits and losses were his own. With that mindset, he worked conscientiously so that the money he earned exceeded his costs.

Beyond teaching me, my father-in-law assured me that I had the qualities to make my own way in the world: a business acumen and work ethic to match. Over and over, patiently and confidently, he urged me to think of myself as more than another man's laborer. "Son," he said, "you already have the seeds planted; just fertilize them and watch them grow!"

In 1973, when he was only fifty-two years of age, the kind man and great teacher lost his life to lung cancer. That same year, Metro Waterproofing celebrated its first anniversary. Pops lived just long enough to see his pupil succeed on his own. A great mentor, my father-in-law realized that independence was the greatest gift he could have given me; in turn, I share the credit for my success with him.

The Order of Leading

Learning to take orders and gaining experience from each task are insights that prepare a person to lead. That's why I would be the first one to volunteer for every job, including when I was in the military. What I did—picking up paper, cleaning the bathrooms, or any other menial task—didn't matter. Each little job had a purpose. I knew if I volunteered,

I'd soon be the leader, the guy in charge. To better my chances, I took each one of the classes related to leadership training that I could during my military career.

Later in life, after succeeding on my own, I've emphasized one point, over and over: to step up! I've strived to instill the importance of taking the initiative when teaching high school students about entrepreneurship. (I've coached young people in Atlanta schools who participate in Junior Achievement as well as students enrolled in our local high schools in Lawrenceville.) "You'll double your salary!" I tell them.

Expecting a more take-charge attitude among students in entrepreneur classes, I like to ask them to tell me who in the room is running for class president. Of all students, I tell them that they should be the ones who have something to say and want to be heard. I also strongly support a curriculum that encourages students to speak out.

I'd love to see more students running for president—or any other leadership role—of their class or club. More adults should also step up at work and in their clubs and organizations. The ones who volunteer for leadership, whether for their church, Rotary Club, or P.T.A., are more likely to be successful in many aspects of their lives.

Too many young people are afraid of taking chances, standing out from the crowd, possibly making mistakes, and having their peers ridicule them. The more mistakes we'll make, however, the better we'll be because of what we've learned. That's why they put erasers on pencils!

I was a country boy yet never cared what other people thought of me. They could say or think whatever they wanted. No one had to tell me I was uneducated or the illogical one to take a job. I knew and volunteered anyway.

The more you lead, the more you learn. Leadership is the root of all growth. Taking responsibility further changes your condition from feeling and being controlled by others to feeling and being in control.

Taking the Driver's Seat

I WAS SIXTEEN WHEN I moved in with my brother and sister-in-law, and went to work for Mr. Hardee. A year and a half later, after reading an article in a newspaper about the chance to travel by selling magazine subscriptions, I left home to see the world. After thirty days, while in Dallas, Texas, I was so homesick that I thumbed all the way back to Greenville, North Carolina.

Although my time there was short, while in Dallas, I met an angelic lady, who gave me a whole new perspective on Christianity and faith. As I stood on her doorstep, she looked at me with compassionate eyes and asked, "Have you ever read chapter three from the book of John?" She was referring to part of the New Testament which relays what it means to be *born again*—making the scriptures real and applicable to everyday life by developing a personal relationship with God. I hadn't, so when I returned to my dingy hotel room, I read that portion of the gospel. Suddenly, I understood why I had felt so unfilled in life. I didn't need to travel the world to find what I had been missing. The emptiness had been inside me. Something told me to return home to figure out where I needed to go from there.

Back in my home state, with just a few dollars in my pocket, I began a new job with J. A. Jones Construction, formerly a worldwide organization that operated for over one hundred years. Working on the construction of a fiberboard plant didn't excite me, so I left after three months. I was back in Selma, NC, and my parents, who were struggling financially and had no other place to live, moved in with me.

My parents lost everything in 1955 from what, I was always told, would be the first civil lawsuit in North Carolina. The year before, my brother Doug, seventeen at the time, was driving his 1954 Ford 110 miles per hour with seven friends in the car. Well, they crashed. Incredibly, no one was seriously hurt, even though the vehicle turned over seven times and everyone was thrown out. One girl, however, suffered considerable damage to her kneecap and underwent surgery to have it replaced.

My father paid the hospital bill, which was the way decent people took responsibility back then. He thought that was the end of it, but the girl's parents sued for $50,000. The figure may as well have been in the millions. My parents didn't have that kind of money, so Dad was forced to sell everything—his horses, his mules, his tractors. The girl's family even took the hogs from the pen and the chickens from the yard.

My parents had farmed their entire lives up to then, so the lawsuit left them with no home and no livelihood. Since neither could read nor write, the only jobs they could get were menial. At fifty-five, mother was cleaning houses and ironing clothes to earn money. My dad, fifty-eight, would find work painting and doing yardwork. I took them in and paid up what they owed in Social Security taxes so they could eventually draw Social Security checks. I also paid most of the rent on a house we shared. For eight years, until Sandra and I married, I gave them the cream—the first portion of everything I earned—and continued helping them until Dad died at eighty and Mom at ninety.

As a young man, nevertheless, always looking for ways to better myself, I once again needed to leave home. At the age of eighteen, I enlisted in the military, where I spent three years. For two years and four months, I was stationed in Germany. When my stint was over, I was so happy to be back in the United States that after landing in New York City, I kissed the ground!

Upon returning to civilian life, I took a job with Glenoit Fabrics, which made imitation fur. The lifelong benefit of that job was my meeting Sandra from passing the produce stand that she operated for her father on my way to work.

Instantly attracted to her, I asked her out, but she didn't want to date me! Thankfully, my future mother-in-law convinced her daughter to give me a chance because, as she said, I was hardworking. (After graduating high school, Sandra also went to work for the mill until we got married.)

No doubt, I was hardworking, but Pops, my father-in-law, motivated me to do more. In addition to working at the mill, I earned extra money on my own by selling sweet potatoes door to door on Saturdays. I'd purchase thirty-one bushels, which I'd sell within five hours and net thirty-one dollars. After Pops let me borrow his truck twice to haul my produce, I bought my own—a new blue and white Chevrolet.

Since I was working the third shift from four in the afternoon to midnight at the mill, I earned extra cash during regular hours with my hauling operations. In a side business, I collected discarded pasteboard from two different mills, tied it all up in bundles, and hauled the loads to the paper mill to recycle in manufacturing.

I also used my truck to pick up and deliver dirt. I'd load the truck with my shovel, and when I arrived at a customer's home, I'd shovel out the soil and then spread it evenly around the yard with a rake. I'd deliver three or four loads on three or four mornings per week for five dollars per load. On average, I'd pocket fifty-five dollars per week, which would be equivalent to more than four hundred dollars today. Focusing on the labor involved in earning the first five dollars, my coworkers would tell me I was crazy. In response, I'd say, "I earned one-third of your salary, tax free, before you even got out of bed!"

I was then hired by Wamsutta Mills to set up a textile plant in Morganton, North Carolina, where I trained and managed thirty employees to run the plant. I excelled and found the work easy, but was bored after one year. I've always had a tremendous amount of energy, so accomplishing the day's task was not enough. I wanted to do more. By wanting to do more, I've achieved more.

Recognizing my ambition, Borge Fabrics offered me a job to a run a factory in Roswell, Georgia. Once I arrived, though, I learned that they wanted me to work on the third shift. Sandra was pregnant, and I didn't want to leave her home alone at night, so within two weeks I quit. That was the only time I quit a job without having a new one waiting, but I readily proceeded with a new plan.

With only the rare exception, you must plan for leaving and for climbing the tree to success.

Following a brief return to North Carolina, I moved Sandra and me to Columbia, South Carolina, where we began transporting tomatoes and other perishable produce from Florida to South Carolina. With the next opportunity, hauling peaches from South Carolina to Raleigh, we moved to Raleigh. Pops and I were selling our produce at farmers' markets, and although profits were slim, we worked quickly to ensure everything remained fresh and to keep turning our inventory. Through our diligence, we attracted restaurant people among other customers, and some would buy the entire load. By hauling and selling 325 bushels or more per day, my father-in-law and I would earn up to $800 apiece per week, which, in 1965, had the buying power of more than $6,000 today.

We decided to get out of the produce business when Theresa, our first child, was born. Driving a milk truck allowed me to keep normal hours, but my income dropped to one hundred dollars per week. I calculated that we needed $150 weekly to live, and that simple equation told me I needed to raise some cash, such as by trading my fancy new Chevrolet Impala for a station wagon.

I've always lived how I've advised others: You have expenses every day, so you need a job every day to meet that responsibility. For a better income, I went to work for General Electric (GE), my first union job. I stayed with the company no more than four months, but the experience with a union operation provided valuable insights in serving my next and final employer, Holbrook Waterproofing.

From the moment that Marcus Holbrook hired me in March of 1966, I worked to learn as much as I could about the waterproofing business and his preferred ways of doing business. He rewarded me with a promotion to foreman within two weeks and the highest salary of any other employee by the third month. Most of all, I had at last found work that ideally suited me. In 1972, when I was well-prepared to run my own operation, I launched Metro Waterproofing. The never-ending challenges to achieve more in the waterproofing business and historical restoration appealed to me. I liked the fact of climbing higher and higher without reaching the top.

The more I did and created, the more I expanded my vision, gaining a view of greater things. I welcomed new opportunities and what others would teach me, but I never let others' ideas about what I could or could not accomplish, or an employer's vague promise, keep me in a role or keep from moving on.

Growing Pains

Marcus Holbrook of Holbrook Waterproofing introduced me to the waterproofing business. The industry creates barriers that prevent water from seeping inside buildings and control where water flows on a property. Practicing my rule of learning as much as I could as quickly as possible about the industry, I chose not to run to the local beer joint after work or to go home to sit in front of the television set. Using my free time productively, I read every piece of literature I could find on caulking and other materials used in the industry.

Until I'd started reading, I didn't even know how to spell *caulk* (I thought the word was c-a-l-k), but soon knew more about the waterproofing process than any other person in the company. I learned what my boss liked, too, and set out to please him by doing my job the way he wanted without his asking. I had been working for him only a few months before becoming a job superintendent. Nothing taught me more than managing.

The Cost of Leroy's Second Chance

Naturally, some of the laborers resented me. Leroy, a seven-year veteran of Holbrook, habitually challenged my authority by missing work altogether or turning up hours late and tipsy from drinking. Allowing him to get away with his misconduct not only compromised my position of authority, but his behavior also put all of us at a disadvantage. The other workers and I couldn't rely on him, so I didn't have a choice but to fire him.

That night, after being fired, a remorseful Leroy visited my hotel room. (We sometimes stayed at hotels while working out-of-town jobs.) Outlining his responsibility to his family, he promised to take his job seriously if I granted him one last chance. He pled so sincerely for his family's sake that I couldn't refuse him. That evening, allowing my heart to rule my head, I rehired Leroy.

To ease the strain of our tense relationship, I started the next day by assigning him the light task of checking the quality of the swinging scaffolding. (If you're doing anything on a swinging stage, such as waterproofing a building's exterior, you check the stability of the temporary structure, which could be several stories off the ground, before spending hours on it at work.) In the meantime, I was getting one crew started in their day of damp proofing the adjacent building. Another crew was mixing caulking. Leroy's job of scanning the rigging required only that he use his eyes and brain. If he had done that to the best of his ability, he wouldn't have broken a sweat.

Standing seven stories above me, he signaled that the rigging was secure. In other words, when we stood on the platform, it would be safe, or that's what Leroy said. We didn't have elevators for our scaffolding back in those days, so after grabbing two buckets of caulking, one for each hand, I entered the building and trudged up six flights of stairs to join Leroy on the scaffold.

The moment I crawled out the window and stepped on the wooden plank outside, I spotted a problem. A wedge of wood, a shim, that held a window frame in place was jutting out. Located as it was above the platform of the scaffold, the shim would obstruct the platform from being raised higher when I got ready to work up the wall. We were seventy feet above the sidewalk, but I was sure-footed and capable of fixing the problem by removing the shim so it would be out of the way.

I needed some room to work, so pulled down on the rope to lower the scaffold. As I did, the outrigger—a support beam for the scaffold—on my side of the platform came loose. Instead of stabilizing the platform, my outrigger popped up and started coming over the top of the scaffold, thereby catapulting me and then Leroy into the air.

Everything Collapsed

The moment I began falling, I started kicking my legs out in front of me to prevent myself from landing on my feet, just like the Army's pre-airborne training had taught me. Had I landed feet first, the force would have caused internal damage; thankfully, my military training had paid off. My descent, nevertheless, was slow enough for my mind and body to absorb the terrified shrieks from all who watched me plummet. Preparing for the worse, I landed. Amazingly, the impact stunned me, but falling seemed to be the worst part of the accident. I immediately reared up on my arms and felt little pain. Suddenly, however, just as I was recovering, the scaffolding came crashing down on me like a thunderbolt.

Leroy came next, landing atop everything. He probably would have been fine had he not touched down on his feet.

After striking me on the face, the scaffold and Leroy pinned me to the earth and produced a shockwave of anger and agony. I remember every second, including bellowing from beneath the wreck. "Get this shit off me!" I screamed. "I gotta get back to work!"

Inconceivably to me, I was about to gain a completely different perspective of my construction site—the inside of Duke University Hospital's ER. Preparing for my work each morning, I had grown accustomed to hearing the uplifting laughter and conversation among nurses on their way to care for patients. During my freefall from the platform, my ears caught the sounds of their screams. Even worse, I would be their next critical patient.

Upon surveying my mangled body, the physicians informed me that I wouldn't be returning to work for a long time. Their grim prognosis explained that the fall had compressed my lowest vertebrae within a quarter of an inch of my pelvis. Such an injury not only threatened paralysis, but virtually guaranteed permanent disability. In fact, the corrective surgery prescribed by the orthopedic surgeon presented three equally likely outcomes: debilitation, paralysis or death.

My immediate future required all the will that I could muster to survive. Immobile in a hospital bed, I had almost 300 stitches in my lacerated face, I could have stuck my finger through a hole in my knee, and my arm was so badly skinned that raw bone was exposed. Since the specialists didn't know the extent of my internal injuries, they wouldn't allow me to take anything stronger for pain than aspirin. When I could not bear the relentless, mind-numbing agony another minute, I begged God to end the ordeal. I prayed for Him to send an angel of death or an angel of mercy.

Nearly mad from the torment, I rang for the nurses incessantly, clutching the call button to me like a lifeline. As the morning waned, however, they stopped answering. The poor staff had no remedy and probably couldn't endure the terrible sight of me sobbing.

A moment of peace arrived when I looked up from my blood-stained gurney and saw my wife. Sandra had been working as Holbrook's bookkeeper, so she was in the

Charlotte office when a member of the crew had called to inform our employer of the incident at the Duke site. Before learning that I was involved, Sandra had watched as Mr. Holbrook received the news and respond by dropping his head. Turning to her, he'd said, "Sandra, go home and pack a bag. It's Clyde."

For two and a half hours, the time it took to travel by car from the company's home office in Charlotte to me in Durham, no one knew how seriously I had been injured. They didn't even know if I'd survived. Thankfully, the Holbrooks had driven Sandra, who still remembers watching the countryside zip past and refusing to imagine the possibility that our future dreams, family included, would never materialize. Instead, she remained firm in her belief that the cocky farm boy who loved her so completely was alive and well in Durham. Otherwise, not only would Sandra have lost her husband, but Theresa, our nine-month-old daughter and first child, sleeping as if nothing threatened the happiness she had known since birth, would have lost her daddy.

Upon catching a glimpse of Sandra's radiant red hair across the emergency room, I felt the recent horror vanish, as if the purest thing in the world—my love for her—had cleansed the room of all fear and pain. With every ounce of gallantry that I could muster, I smiled and told her, "You're beautiful." Immediately, however, the staff, thinking they were doing what was best for me, made the terrible error of forcing her to leave my side when they moved me to my room.

They were concerned that her presence might upset me. The second she left the room, my nightmare resumed.

Fifteen hours into the ordeal, around 11:00 that night, God sent his angel of mercy, a nurse working the night shift. She gingerly entered my room, and before leaving, promised to check on me again as soon as she made her rounds. A few minutes later, she returned and continued to come back every thirty minutes. While the nurse couldn't end my agony, she rolled me onto my side, massaged my back, and softly assured me, "You will be all right." Her low, melodious voice, healing hands, and commitment to soothe and comfort me did more to foster my recovery than all the medicine I received. Again and again, all night long, she gave me a reason to have faith and lulled me to peace.

After that first endless night and its cycles of peace and pain, I knew that I would live. The unanswered question was what kind of life I faced. The medical experts on my case predicted at least four months of recuperation and rehabilitation in the hospital, followed by a lifetime disability. "You'll never be the person you were," one fine doctor told me.

He was right. I would not ever be the same man that I'd been before the fall, but I would not be less abled, as the doc imagined.

Seven days after the preventable accident, they pushed my wheelchair to the door. I struggled out of it, put my feet on the floor, and walked the three steps to the car that would take me home. Once home, I shared Theresa's babysitter while Sandra continued to work at Holbrook. Still, I refused to be treated like a baby. The only baby in our home was Theresa, and as her daddy, my job was to take care of her. With that in mind, I'd motivate myself to get up and move daily by walking to buy Theresa an ice cream cone. I would try to return home before it melted, but my pace was too slow. The ice cream would be dripping all over my hand. At least I tried, and Theresa didn't mind. She loved what was left, each and every day.

Back on the Job

Four weeks later, after growing accustomed to the back brace that enclosed my torso, I was once again on a jobsite. Holbrook had acquired the first electric scaffold in the Southeast, but no one could get it assembled properly. My brother, also working for Holbrook, called me for help. I couldn't reach my feet, so Sandra tied my shoes for me before I left home. Once on the job, still wearing bandages on my face and arm, I agreed when my brother asked me to join him on the scaffold.

We were ten stories up.

To say that I went back to work at little too soon, especially when that meant standing on a platform about one hundred feet off the ground, would be an understatement. My body was shaking so badly that I thought for certain the scaffold would fall, but I stayed on it. After about thirty minutes of standing and trembling, I suddenly became calm. Until then, my brother had been busy caulking, so I got busy. Since I couldn't bend down, he took care of the lower sections and I caulked where I could reach above. Together, he and I caulked ten floors that day.

For eighteen months, I couldn't reach down to tie my shoes. People would have understood if I'd stayed home to recover. My family motivated me to get up rather than accept worker's compensation payments, and I never took a dime of disability insurance. I refused to let someone else support my wife and baby. If anyone was going to provide for my little girl, if only to buy her an ice cream cone, I would be the man.

Thanks to my father's DNA, I was innately fearless about heights. His grandparents were Cherokee Indians, and as a boy, I enjoyed hearing the Native American folklore that told of human flight. I'd dreamed that I, too, could soar through the sky. Getting back up there was less of a leap for me than it would have been for someone less naturally inclined to climb.

No one would argue that I had spunk, but I was no Superman. As the Duke physician had warned me, the fall had made me a different man.

Two months after being discharged from the hospital, I was startled awake in the middle of the night by my own screaming. With certainty, I believed that daggers were grinding every millimeter of my spinal column. Sandra frantically grabbed the phone to call 9-1-1, and the paramedics were soon rushing me to the hospital. There I learned that the sensation of being tortured meant that my nerves were rejuvenating—a sure sign that my back was healing. "They're growing pains," the ER doctor said.

In addition to accompanying my physical renewal, my suffering caused me to grow spiritually. I had grown to cherish every day that I lived, embracing the smallest pleasure and beauty as the miracles they were. All these years later, not a day passes without my feeling sharp, radiating pains to remind me of how delicate and fleeting the miracles of life can be. Such pain has been a small price for gaining wisdom and depth of character.

The Upside

Going back to work instead of waiting around at home further propelled my career. After that first day of waterproofing ten stories of brick with my brother, I called Holbrook to update him on the progress. That's when he sent me to another job—the VA hospital at Salisbury, North Carolina. Still unable to tie my own shoes and struggling to get in the truck, I traveled 145 miles to the site. Once on the job, I could walk only one hundred feet at a time before taking a rest, so I'd carry a straight-back chair and walking stick to work. The need to sit, however, gave me a chance to observe and advise the workers.

The project entailed historical renovation, a new area for me, so I began learning everything I could. I loved the work and enjoyed becoming an expert in the field. From my continued education and experience, I eventually wrote the first specifications related to historical renovation by outlining the process—replacing brick and broken concrete, caulking and sealing, and protecting the structure with the appropriate waterproofing—for the University of Georgia.

I refused to let a tragedy turn me into a tragic person. Eventually, I also recognized that God had put my body out of commission for a reason: I had to start using my mind, not my back, and that's when I began to grow into a new person.

Sadly, Leroy allowed the fall to take him down and out. Granted, his body suffered greatly from serious injuries to his bladder and kidneys, but his doctors and nurses expressed to me that Leroy would survive, if only he had the will to live. He didn't. After ninety days in the hospital, Leroy gave up and died. It's impossible to know all that was going through his mind, but Sandra and I seemed to be his only visitors. Disregarding his responsibility for the accident, we just tried to love him and treat Leroy as we'd want to be treated. Seeing that he was lonely, a distance from home and family, we did what we could to encourage him. He just didn't have the fight.

Moving on Down the Road

The lingering pain in my back from the fall made me more acutely aware of my physical limitations. On top of that, wearing the cumbersome brace (I still wear a brace when pain tells me I need the support) that was required to rehabilitate my spine made strenuous manual labor impossible. Before, I'd motivate my crews by jumping into muddy foundations and onto rooftops, inspiring them to work as hard as I did. Since I could no longer show them by example, I had to cultivate different approaches. I used logic and emotion.

As it turned out, I had a talent for bringing out the best in people. My crews outperformed the others, and when our reputation for superior quality spread, building contractors requested me and my team by name. Additionally, many—namely, my boss and customers—counted on my knowledge of the technical and economic intricacies of the industry to develop best practices and to guide them.

From my role of the diligent, trustworthy foreman to the manager with a depth of industry knowledge, I relied on my brain to succeed. By earning responsibility and respect, I gained independence.

Promoted to Georgia

In the late 1960s and early 1970s, when Atlanta was rapidly growing with the promise of becoming one of America's most important cities, Holbrook sent me to the region as a problem solver. I'd been working in Virginia when he presented the challenge to reverse a bad situation in Georgia. All the money that had been budgeted for the project was spent, but the union workers in Atlanta still had twenty-six floors to waterproof before finishing the job. To prepare me, my boss gave me a book of union guidelines. The book didn't help, but previously, over three short months, I'd worked with organized labor at General Electric (GE), and that little bit of experience of listening to people's concerns and laying out the facts so they'd cooperate was invaluable.

Holbrook called me in Virginia on a Thursday to be in Atlanta on the upcoming Monday morning. I didn't have much time to prepare to leave, but no one intended me to remain in Georgia. As it turned out, I had everything straightened out and running smoothly with time to spare, so I asked Holbrook if I could stay and solicit new business. As I picked up contracts to work on schools and federal projects, Holbrook agreed that I should open a new office, Holbrook Waterproofing of Georgia.

I not only opened the office, but I also operated as the general manager, salesman and laborer. Sandra, of course, relocated with me and assumed the secretarial duties.

In January 1969, when we moved to Duluth, Georgia, our youngest, Kenneth, was only thirty days old. Sandra drove him and Theresa in the station wagon. I had eighteen-month-old Michael and two dogs with me in a truck with no seatbelts and missing pieces of floorboard. When we looked down, we could see Interstate 85 passing beneath our feet. The drive itself should have been an indication that we were in for a ride!

Soon after I moved to Georgia, I had a terrible bout with kidney stones. As the general manager, I couldn't stop working, so I ran the company from a hospital bed for seventeen days. Don Ross, a friend from my church, would come every day to visit me. (Not so many years later, after my business suffered a great loss, he also lent me money without any question of when I'd repay him.)

The next year, I started taking evening classes in blueprints to read them correctly, drafting to draw detailed plans, and management. The benefits from that investment were tremendous, although many in the same situation would have quit the program. On top of putting in a full day of work and studying at lunch or when possible, which is not unusual for people attending night school, I was often racing three-year-old Theresa to the hospital in the middle of the night because of her asthma attacks. Sandra would stay home with our toddler and baby boys. Frequently, the doctor would admit Theresa for three or four days until she recovered. My sleep would amount to catnaps in the rocking chair.

Meanwhile, I was busy at work and confident that the company would prosper under my management. It sure did, and I had purchased seventeen percent of the business in stock. My compensation should have included that percentage of the net profit: $40,000 then, which would have the spending power of $240,000 as of this writing. When Mr. Holbrook failed to mail my check, I told Sandra I was ready to move on. I would not be satisfied until I answered only to myself. I had always known that I was meant to be my own boss, but for a period, I'd accepted the authority of my superiors—my father, Wilbur Hardee, the Army, my father-in-law, and Marcus Holbrook—to learn from them.

Leading by example, Sandra's dad taught the most about business, yet he didn't know how to read or write. Mainly, he motivated me to go out on my own. He'd say, "You can outwork, outthink, and outtalk all of them!" While I couldn't have said that my apprenticeships were over, as I have continued to learn from others my entire life, I was ready then for the next step. I had worked in the metropolitan area long enough to understand the market. I knew how to build strong business relationships.

Credit Lost and Gained

Sandra and I had moved from the first home we'd purchased in Duluth, Georgia, to the next home we bought in Lawrenceville. After assessing the risk, I gambled our home and other assets, totaling all that I had worked for over the past thirty years to ensure a comfortable future for my family through a business of my own. Working together as partners, Sandra and I launched Metro Waterproofing in January of 1972. I did not build the company on my own. Through the years, Sandra's diligence in managing the books and money was integral to our success. My brother Doug also joined us from the first day.

Our original investment included the equity in our home, or $6,000, plus every cent in our savings. In addition, I bought the first month of materials for $14,000 on credit. Quickly, I learned a lesson in credit. As an employee of Holbrook, I could borrow $10,000 from the bank based on my reputation alone. The day I left Holbrook to open a new company, I didn't have a dime of credit. Bankers flatly told me I would fail. Who could blame them? The $18,000, including overhead costs, that we started out owing was significant; the sum would equate to $109,000 today.

I never made the mistake of overestimating net profits by underestimating my overhead costs, which are the expenses required to keep a business running. New entrepreneurs often fail by making that error. In comparison, I had a clear plan and realistic goals. Taking care of my employees was my priority from the first job on, and my obligation for others quickly expanded. We went from having three people working for us to employing eight by the end of the first month. To ensure I made payroll, I drove to my customer in Toccoa, Georgia, to pick up that first check.

During the first forty-eight days, Sandra and I lived from hand to mouth. Along with paying our workers, we had to buy the essentials to keep our office running. Among those items were a cheap typewriter (the only way to write a professional correspondence before computers), a basic calculator (another ancient tool), and a plain desk. The desk now graces the foyer of our lake house as a monument to Metro Waterproofing's humble beginnings and a testament to maintaining a positive cash flow by not spending money we didn't have on things we didn't absolutely need.

At that time in our lives, Sandra was busy mothering our three young children, but we couldn't afford to hire someone to run the office. Therefore, she handled the operations from her sewing room in our basement. I managed our crew, including my brother Doug and our first employee Jim. A used pickup truck with one ladder served as our transportation equipment.

While the sum of it all doesn't seem like much now, the full responsibility was tremendous at the time. Every job bore my company's name and directly reflected on me. I refused to rest until our customers recognized the quality and efficiency of our work. That commitment to excellence gradually rewarded me.

Like most startups, a small contractor relies on word-of-mouth advertising within the industry. I knew that if I performed one job well, then my customer would tell ten or so people. If I did one job poorly, then my customer would tell one hundred. By never giving a customer a reason to complain, which would have jeopardized Metro's reputation, we grew rapidly—so rapidly, in fact, that we had to buy an office and a storage barn (for materials and equipment) within the first year.

Our growth streak continued for fourteen demanding but wonderful years, and by 1986, our tiny company occupied an entire city block in Scottdale, Georgia, an unincorporated community adjacent to Decatur, Georgia. We also employed over one hundred men and women. Upon arriving at work every morning, I would view the compound before me as a concrete testament to my hard work and independence. The buildings were also home to a community, the family of people who encompassed Metro Waterproofing.

In October of that amazing year, all that we had labored to achieve burned to the ground.

Ashes to Assets

Never a good sleeper, I had been dreaming only an hour at 1:30 a.m., when the phone by my bedside rang. A ring at that time of morning always sounds ominous, so I expected bad news. "You better get down here!" a voice shouted. "Metro's on fire!"

My wife and I sped in the car down Stone Mountain Highway and East Ponce De Leon Avenue towards Scottdale, while assuring one another that everything would be all right. We hoped against hope that our optimism was warranted, but when we arrived, the sirens and flashing lights said otherwise. The entire block seemed to be engulfed in fire as flames roared into the night sky. With our faces burning from inferno's intense heat, Sandra and I stood crying and holding hands, silent and helpless. We watched Metro Waterproofing topple into a smoldering heap of black ash.

When we gained enough composure to see beyond the initial disaster, we found some words to console one another. We were certain our insurance would restore the business that had sustained us for so long, but some shocking information slashed our one shred of optimism. To make the policy appealing to us and thereby keep us as clients, our insurance broker had changed the terms without our consent. He wrote us a policy that cost us less upfront because it covered only half of the business. Thanks to his terrible judgment, in just one night, we lost more than one million dollars in capital.

Following that crippling news, our bond company, which assumed the risk for our operations, deemed us to be a bad risk and denied us surety bonds. Such bonds would have guaranteed our customers that we had the financial assurances in place to accomplish the work as promised. Companies that provided our materials likewise refused to extend credit to us, so we had to buy everything with cash. That's a tough position in industrial construction. Projects often take months or years to complete, so we generally wait for payments while work is underway. On top of the credit issues facing us, we also found out that our company owed $375,000 in back taxes to the Internal Revenue Service (IRS).

After I negotiated with IRS agents in person, they gave us a break by deducting all the interest and penalties, reducing our debt to the principal amount of $171,000. From that point on, we had to pay $5,000 per month in interest. We met another obstacle when an agent reviewed our financial records and thought we were hiding money. To force us to pay up, she attempted to put a lien on our possessions. Speaking on our behalf, the president of our bank explained to her that if they took our assets, our business would fail and the IRS would never receive what we owed. He changed her mind, so we continued paying the debt on schedule, finally catching up after several years.

Rumors of our impending bankruptcy nearly wiped out the positive word-of-mouth network that had built Metro's reputation. Nevertheless, I was determined to restore what we'd lost. Getting past temporary moments of feeling hopeless, I'd remember an angel (a heaven-sent messenger) I'd met on the night of the fire.

Angels in the Ashes

The angel came in the form of an arson inspector, who led me through the rubble after the firefighters had extinguished the flames. As he pointed out signs that the building had been destroyed intentionally, I noticed that the man kept dropping his notepad. I assumed he was a little clumsy from a chill in the cold October air. When he finished his assessment, and pulled off his glove, I learned the truth. The inspector had no fingers on one hand. He had lost the digits and the use of that hand in a prior fire. Even so, he had mustered the courage to carry on. He not only kept working, but continued to fight the element that had permanently maimed him.

Left standing there with the audacity to mourn something I could replace, I looked down at my own hands. As if seeing them for the first time, I realized they had built my company the first time and they could do it again. Therefore, when people wondered if bankruptcy might be the soundest option for us, I replied, "You don't know the man that I am!"

With my pronouncement, I refused to go home that night. Bed and sleep were not on my agenda. Instead, driven to resurrect the ruins, I went to work that second. I grabbed a door that the fire had spared and balanced it atop concrete blocks to make a desk. Later, the phone company ran a line straight from the telephone pole to the door. My makeshift office was ready for business. Incredibly, too, Metro Waterproofing managed to cover eighty percent of its jobs that day!

Miraculously, Sandra also found two accounts receivable journals in the ashes that had not been destroyed. In those days, we didn't have our business on computers with records safely backed up on a cloud, so recovering those actual books helped us rebuild Metro Waterproofing. Everyone pitched in, along with Sandra and the children. Theresa was pregnant with her second child, due in January, and she and Myron, her husband, stayed up most evenings until midnight to take care of the billing.

Losing faith in our ability to survive, most of our former allies and associates would abandon us. On the day of the fire, however, Don Ross, my friend, arrived on the spot. Another real angel in my life, he wordlessly handed me an envelope that contained $10,000 in cash, his entire inheritance. Without expressing a single condition or requesting any promise that I would repay him, Don offered me one of the kindest gifts I've ever received: his faith in me. Although I'd invested many wasted hours trying to teach him how to fish and operate a barbecue grill to little avail, I'd spent my time wisely in choosing a best friend. His faith absolutely restored my confidence when almost everyone else seemed to question it.

Investing in the recovery of Metro demanded that Sandra and I relive the anxiety of losing everything we owned, yet the stakes were much higher than when we first launched the company. Starting out, we had so little to lose. Starting over, we had to mortgage our entire estate for every dollar the bank would lend. After one loan, we had to return to the bank for a second, and the officer advised me to ask for all I could get. "Clyde," he warned sternly, "this is the last time." Before the fire, bankers had begged for my patronage.

For the first year since opening Metro Waterproofing, the company lost money. On top of recovering from the fire, we struggled to pay the exorbitant interest on our loans. Still, we did what we could to reward our deserving employees, although we could no longer hand out lavish bonuses and gifts. Giving each a twenty-dollar bill at Christmas was the most we could afford, but they gratefully accepted and stuck by us.

Ultimately, Metro's destruction became our salvation. Before, we had grown away from our roots, and the crisis reminded us of our beginnings. As a resurrected company, we rediscovered our work ethic and faith, the seeds of our original success. With a renewed spirit, we gained ground on our loans and repaid the debt. Stronger and wiser from surviving the fire, we overcame other obstacles more easily without losing our momentum.

Survival breeds strength. Often, devastation propels us to our greatest heights by allowing us to demonstrate our courage and utilize powerful reserves that we never realized we possessed. Had I never fallen on the Duke jobsite, I probably wouldn't have acknowledged that I was more than a plowboy with a strong back or that I had a head for business and a yearning for independence. Had Metro Waterproofing not burned, then the company might have continued to veer from our original principles and grow out of control.

Most of all, if everything had been easy, I would not have paid attention to the angels or appreciated what is most precious in life.

Something Lost, Something Gained

My injuries from falling off the scaffolding marked the first time I was deemed totally disabled. The second time occurred in 1990. I had just purchased a new Lincoln Town Car and, as usual, I had it out on the road to help someone on a Saturday. For my good deed, I had to drive to Villa Rica, Georgia, about an hour and a half each way from my home in Lawrenceville.

On the way back, I was traveling Highway 78, about twenty minutes away from home, when I called Sandra to get some steaks ready to grill. Soon after, a young lady made an illegal turn at Lake Lucerne Road. Because of her action, a young man driving a Toyota pickup truck knocked me 125 feet down the highway. The impact was so hard that it sling-shot her across 78. She ended up on Lake Lucerne Bridge, and I landed on the Yellow River Bridge. Although my cell phone, which was connected to the car, ended up in pieces, it still worked. I called Sandra again, this time to tell her to forget about the steaks; I'd been in an accident and needed her to meet me.

When the police and ambulance arrived, everyone thought I was just about dead. They rushed me to the closest hospital, Eastside Medical Center, where I learned that the wreck had messed up my neck and one of my knees. My third vertebra and my jawbone were broken. Still, they sent me home later that day.

Two days later, I was in bed when I heard what sounded like the alarm going off and thought someone was breaking into the house. As soon as I got out of bed, I fell to floor. That would be the start of a year-long ordeal of seeing doctors at Emory Hospital, losing one-hundred percent of my hearing in my right ear, and having my jawbone rebuilt with nine pins implanted in my jaw.

After a few years, I began to have abscesses in my ear drum, and my doctor deemed they were coming from the pins. The plan was to remove each of the pins and rebuild the jawbone and gums. That turned into a three-year ordeal with my returning every three or four months for an operation to remove teeth and replace them with implants. At one time, the pain was so great that I had to take a year recess before I could go back and finish the process.

The young lady who caused the accident and the young man involved were less grateful over their outcomes. Seeing me as a wealthy man, they thought I was crooked because I had to sue their insurance companies to cover my hospital bills. Together, they had only $65,000 in insurance, and my hospital bills totaled $58,000. That amount was small in comparison to the $125,000 it cost me to redo my mouth, which I paid.

My attorneys wanted me to sue them for a half-million dollars for loss of business, but I am not a person who believes in suing and messing up young people's lives. Without that young boy and girl ever knowing it, I granted them a free life.

I was granted a successful recovery. I'm grateful to say that for many years I have been able to eat anything I've wanted without toothaches or other problems. Thank God for implants and good doctors!

The incident was also another example of how a tragedy in my life turned to greatness.

The first year of that ordeal, I was away from Metro so much of the time that the company lost money. After an adjustment period, Metro started to grow at a rapid pace because the accident forced me to release responsibility. Before, I had been trying to do too much on my own. After, I had to turn to other people. I even hired a chauffeur to drive me to work for a year. The timing was also perfect. The event happened when Michael first came to work, followed by Kenneth in 1991, so my backing off created a great learning opportunity for them.

The American Work Ethic

No matter how long they lived in this country, generations of Americans grew up with a clear understanding of how the system ran: *if you don't work, you don't eat.*

That principle changed when some people began to believe the system should be free to them.

With every generation, parents complain about their children lacking the kind of work ethic that motivated them. Criticisms of that nature often come from those who don't relate well to the societal changes that affect the way people work. Some don't approve of the cultural transformations. Others have a hard time accepting innovation. One generation, for example, might claim that people with office jobs couldn't possibly work as hard as those laboring in a field all day. The next generation might contend that people working remotely from home couldn't possibly spend as many hours on the job as those who go to offices each day.

Unlike them, I focus on the positive developments. I praise my children's generation for several of their qualities:

their ability to work in teams; their acceptance of people who differ from them; their higher education. Giving each of my children a chance to run the company, I have watched them all grow in their respective roles. Working collaboratively, they have further grown Metro Waterproofing beyond my expectations.

At the risk of sounding old and crotchety, however, I do believe that the overall work ethic in America has suffered an astounding decline that threatens our country.

Time will tell if upcoming generations continue to enjoy more comfortable lifestyles than the one I had as a child and young adult. Up to now, they have lived quite well. Even poor households tend to own luxuries, including televisions and other gadgets. Therefore, the youngest in the workforce (or kids who are old enough to work) generally do not have a true sense of wealth's origin: hard work. As such, they believe they are entitled to the freedoms and comforts that prior generations of men and women earned by the sweat of their brow.

To instill a work ethic, parents should give their children age-appropriate chores, like making their beds and cleaning their rooms. Adults, too, benefit from performing such tasks. By hiring others to do every bit of work we don't much enjoy, we spoil ourselves and our children. Moreover, the attitude that we shouldn't force ourselves to perform such tasks is ruining our country. Neglecting to take responsibility for little jobs creates big problems in many aspects of life.

Instilling Accountability

By the time our three—Kenneth, Michael and Theresa—were six years old, they were given chores. They were also responsible for setting their alarm clocks to wake up on time. On the rare morning when they needed an incentive to rise and shine, I'd trigger the smoke detector. No one could rest in bed with that terrible sound blaring through the house! They also knew what it was like to wake up to cold water pouring over their heads while I sang, "Rise and shine!" We hardly ever had to wake them during their school years, including on Saturdays, when we expected our children to be up by 8:00 a.m.

On top of that, they rarely missed a day of school or work. From kindergarten through his senior year of high school, Kenneth had perfect attendance. Michael missed only five days. They especially knew to be on time, and in our family, that meant arriving fifteen minutes early—a well-established behavior by the time they graduated and held jobs in our company.

As little children, they also got themselves dressed in the morning and ready for bed at night on their own; they kept their bedrooms and bathrooms clean; when they appeared for breakfast, they respectfully helped their mother as needed. While I was working long hours in the business, Sandra would organize chores for the kids after school. Even a small child can pick up sticks outside or wash the cars. When ours were seven, they were already riding the lawnmower and using the edger under careful supervision. Other boys and girls in the neighborhood would see how busy they were and ask, "Do y'all do anything else but work?"

They weren't just busy; our three understood that we expected them to do their jobs well—to the best of their ability. Partly motivated by a healthy dose of fear (they were a little afraid of my punishment), they usually did not disappoint us. Even if they wouldn't admit it, the work also gave them a sense of self-satisfaction.

Once, when the boys had been told to gather up sticks that were scattered across the yard, they were entirely pleased with an impressive pile they'd made with the hundreds they'd collected. However, when I arrived home, I found quite a few stragglers still left here and there on the lawn. Most parents would have praised their kids for a task well done, which Sandra and I often did, but in this instance, I wanted to teach them to fulfill their obligations. They needed to finish their chore before dinner.

"He who you check performs!" I would tell them, and they knew I would be checking.

I also noted their limitations but pushed each one to acquire and master new skills. Although the boys used to fight over who would operate the riding lawn mower, which was easier than hand-trimming the shrubs with the shears and more fun than sweeping the cuttings from the driveway and curb, they each went through a training period before learning to use it properly.

Theresa never quite got to be a confident driver. I assigned her to the mover anyway, and she ran over my prized Liriope, an ornamental grass that beautified an area of the yard. With that, I learned a lesson: Theresa should never operate the riding mower!

Kenneth did the same thing when he was first learning the ins and outs of the mower. He leveled the Liriope *and* some bushes, and then worried about telling me for fear that I'd get upset with him. Instead, I showed him that it was not the end of the world. Together, we replanted everything and replaced the pine straw around the bushes.

Not to be left out, Michael ran the mower into the fence, which belonged to our next-door neighbor. The good fellow ran to the rescue, kindly helping Michael free the machine from the rubbish. We couldn't salvage the fence, so Michael and I helped take it down. Unlike the woman who had previously lived in the home and wanted the barrier to keep the kids out, our new neighbor liked children. He found no need to rebuild the fence, and we all became great friends.

Things happen, and my kids learned that you just have to rebuild or move on. The mower and other outdoor chores taught some great lessons to us all.

Sure, we could have hired others to provide all kinds of services, but Sandra and I knew that our children needed to do the little things that would grow into big things. Teaching them the value of work, we would award each child an allowance with an incentive plan—more work, more pay! Their earnings, however, came with responsibilities. Each child was required to tithe, giving God (charity) ten percent. Eighty percent had to go into savings, leaving ten percent to spend. They've all tithed their entire life and consequently have been blessed with good health and good children of their own.

I want to note here that Sandra and I didn't just teach our kids to write out checks. Making a difference in people's lives is more often about doing, sometimes getting your hands dirty. When they were boys, for instance, Michael, Kenneth and I put a swing set together to fulfill a request from a child with cancer through the Make-A-Wish Foundation. As they worked up a sweat, my sons realized that the sick child would have traded places with them in a second, and they were grateful for the experience.

That's what it takes: building a work ethic during the early years to take through life.

Instilling Confidence

When Theresa, Michael and Kenneth entered middle school, they began working at Metro Waterproofing. They did whatever the adults required of them in the warehouse. One of their first jobs was to pick up Coke bottles that the workers had left around Metro's yard. I didn't pay them much, but as much as they worked, my children were the richest kids in their grade. They were among the most confident, too.

Many parents end up spending a fortune on their children's fundraisers for clubs and schools because they buy up all the raffle tickets, cookies and magazines that their boys and girls should be striving to sell to their neighbors, friends and extended family. Sandra and I generously supported their schools and clubs, but they knew better than to ask us to make their lives easier. "Hit the streets," I'd say. Theresa remembers doing such a great job one year that she sold 200 boxes of Girl Scout Cookies. Later required to deliver each box on her own, she'd tell you that selling had been the easy part!

I would, of course, step in when they needed me. Mike and Kenneth, for instance, hit the streets to secure a high number of generous pledges for a bike-a-thon on behalf of the Cystic Fibrosis Foundation. They next went the distance by biking thirty-five miles. The total each person owed the charity would be the individual's pledge in dollars or cents per mile times thirty-five. From their efforts, my sons raised more for the fundraiser than any of the other participants, which earned them a trophy and a story in the local paper. Most underestimated my sons' drive and pledged more generously than they would have, but everyone paid up—except one of our neighbors. He refused to honor his commitment.

When Kenneth told me, I said, "Let's go, boy!" We went right to the man's home. Face-to-face with him, I asked, "Is that what you're going teach a young boy?" I shamed him into paying. Possibly, he was a little frightened of my temper. Even more relevant is that I didn't handle this alone, but rather provided an example to Kenneth of how to stand up for himself.

In some cases, I coached them along. Other times, I let them figure it all out on their own.

The day that Kenneth came home with his learner's permit to drive, I handed him the keys my Lincoln Continental. Did I mention that my bass boat was hitched to it? I had a confidence-building lesson, not a joyride, in mind for my teenager. He'd never had his foot on the gas pedal in his life, but that didn't stop me from putting him behind the driver's seat. "Come on," I said, "You're going to drive me to Lake Lanier." Adding to the pressure, his young friend sat in the backseat and went with us! I knew we'd all be fine, especially Kenneth. Traffic was light, and I was right there beside my son, speaking calmly to him throughout the trip.

Theresa remembers me calling her at home to say that her mom was just leaving the office. Nearly dinnertime,

I told her to start making the meal. She had assisted and watched her mother cook, but my daughter didn't know what she would serve or how she would go about preparing each dish from scratch. Theresa put her mind and hands to work and figured it out.

Teaching Cause and Effect

Providing the tools that allow children to figure things out is essential. If I wasn't preaching to them, I was teaching my children a life lesson. "Come here. Let me teach you something to teach your kids someday," I would say. The task might have been as simple as changing a lightbulb, but many grown men and women don't know how to do basic chores like that; no one ever showed them.

My determination to teach my children the art of living—reaping the fruits of their labor—kept me from hiring a lawn service while they were growing up. By habit, Sandra and I continued to mow and edge after they went to college. I should also note that those were the years when we were working fourteen-hour days to rebuild Metro Waterproofing after the devastating fire that literally took the company down to the ground. Still, I found the hours, even when I didn't have any free time on Saturday to mow the grass. Sandra and I were committed to attending both of our boys' weekend football games, so with no other breaks in my schedule, I moved my outdoor chores to Thursday night, after work.

We always made their functions our priority. At one point, while Kenneth was still playing football for Central Gwinnett High School and Michael was a starter for Appalachian State University in Boone, North Carolina, we would go to Kenneth's Friday evening game and then immediately drive at least four and a half hours to Boone to watch Michael play. We also traveled by car to away games. Driving to Wheeling, West Virginia, took ten hours each way without any stops. Nevertheless, Sandra and I missed only one game during the four years that Michael played.

Complicating our tight schedule were the shorter days of fall, when the sun would go down earlier in the evening. Running out of daylight, I'd have to turn on the car lights so I could see what I was doing. *What was I thinking?* Finally, as I finished up one night in the dark, Sandra pointed out to me that the kids were gone, and I was not using my time wisely. I could at last hire someone to deal with the yard!

Left with riding and push lawnmowers and edgers that I would no longer use, I donated them to St. Matthews Episcopal Church in Snellville. The church had a lean-to behind the main building, so I stored everything under that little shed. Apparently, the easily accessible equipment presented a great temptation to at least one thief. The first lot was stolen, so I replaced it all with new equipment. That, too, was stolen, so I purchased yet another set of machines. I also bought a trailer to transport the items to and from my home and church until I could build a secure structure. Clyde's Fortress, made of concrete and steel, deterred future thieves and still stands!

As it turned out, hauling the mowers back and forth granted an opportunity for me to motivate a young man who was not my child. Driving the Continental with the trailer behind me, I stopped at a station for gas. The fellow sized up the situation—a luxury car pulling lawn equipment—and approached me. "I have been thinking of getting into that business," he said. "You must be doing well."

"If you work twenty-four hours a day," I replied, "you can make a good living." Chuckling to myself, I purposely didn't leave him with the impression that landscaping was easy. Making a good living is anything but.

Though not without our own faults, those of us born soon after the Great Depression (the period from 1929 to 1939, when people were so poor, even farmers couldn't afford the cost of harvesting their crops and left them dying in the field) know this quite well. We understood that we had to work if we wanted to eat. That principle made my generation the most industrious and successful in America's history.

Where's the motivation to succeed when men and women figure out that they can put food on the table and live more comfortably by going on Welfare than by working?

Here's the Deal

My generation's parents fought World War II—a bloody, global battle—to protect the liberties we have today. Some say the tremendous spending to fund a war that sent millions of young American men overseas put an end to the Great Depression. Others believe that the economy more greatly benefitted from people and governments cutting back and wasting less. Also, as the war ended, the government loosened regulations so that businesses faced fewer obstacles to start up and expand. Taking advantage of the opportunity when they returned home, many soldiers exercised their freedom to launch their own companies that provided goods, services and jobs for their communities.

In part, civilians also crawled out of poverty by taking advantage of President Franklin Roosevelt's New Deal, the country's most far-reaching program of national subsidies and entitlements up to that point in history. Although economists have since debated the question of whether the government's investment improved or slowed the nation's financial recovery, unlike modern welfare programs that pay people to sit around, this setup helped citizens who were willing to work.

The millions of people who gained employment through the Works Progress Administration, or WPA, dug ditches, built roads and constructed bridges. The Farm Bureau, in turn, gave farmers free land, but only if the grower met his quota by working his fields with the intention of producing the highest possible yield.

Today, Americans of all walks of life expect their government to rescue them by supplying housing, food, clothing, healthcare, education and much more for free. Workers also demand that their employers deliver more than a fair compensation. Rather than relishing the freedom to pursue their choice of careers and enjoy the highest standard of living in the world, grown men and women expect their government and bosses to step in as parental substitutes with endless obligations. Like children, they blame their country and their jobs for whatever goes wrong in their personal lives. Too many Americans expect more, but they claim less responsibility and work less productively. They also demonstrate less loyalty to their jobs and to their country.

While laboring on the farm in my youth, I learned that the land returned to us only what we put into it. If bad weather or disease damaged the crop, the land gave less. Either way, if we didn't work, we didn't eat. Many mornings, rising before the sun, we trudged with sore backs and blistered hands into the darkened fields to begin another twelve-hour day. We complained sometimes, but our crops were like sick children requiring constant care. One short day of rest for us might not seem like much in the grand scheme of things, but the consequence of neglecting a single chore could result in a big problem that made the next day's work twice as difficult.

To his credit, my father, Frank Strickland, had a tireless work ethic, and our farm flourished under his direction. At the end of every harvest, other landowners in the area would realize how much greater Dad's yield was than the other tenant farmers' production, and they'd beg for him to work their farms.

His success came from a belief that the land, which fed him, deserved every ounce of his considerable energy and care. Long after other farmers had been using tractors, my father insisted that his old-fashioned methods were better than machines. He wouldn't allow them on his pristine fields of North Carolina tobacco. Worked by man and mule, our rows were immaculate in contrast to neighboring fields that were blotched with mounds of grass. A perfect corridor of bare, swept earth bordered our crops, so the rectangles looked like pictures in rigid frames. The upkeep continued yearlong. During the wet, cold winters, we cut drainage ditch banks with bush axes, and carefully laid tile along their basins so the water would flow off more effectively. My father saw every precise effort, even those that enhanced appearance only, as a testament to his thoroughness.

Few today work as hard as a North Carolina sharecropper to make ends meet—or to gain respect and fair treatment.

The Early Years

Clyde stationed in Germany
and helping Americans -1961

Clyde on his Honda Gold Wing GL 1000

Sandra's Senior Prom with Clyde

Clyde Strickland
is both a philanthropist and profound, faithful teacher, donating his time and talent to making a difference.

Dedicating the Strickland Chapel in the
GWINNETT MEDICAL CENTER

Clyde and Sandra breaking ground for the
< STRICKLAND HEART CENTER

Donation to the Educational Initiative for Georgia
GOVERNOR'S OFFICE

Mark Andol, Clyde, and Ricky Lee

Sharing the message

"MADE IN AMERICA" TEAM

The Value of Fun

Sandra and I had so little money starting out that we had to be frugal. Later, when we could afford far more, we continued our policy of enjoying hobbies and fun times with one another and our children, but we didn't throw away money on stuff for the sake of being extravagant.

Our First Vacation

We married on June 29, 1963. When we went on our honeymoon, we did not know about motels and hotels. Sandra had not stayed in a hotel once in her entire life. After that trip, for the next six years, it was all work. We did not know about vacations. When we took off a day or two, we would visit our parents or in-laws.

In 1969, we went on our first family vacation to the beach. We didn't think we could afford a place right on the beach, so we stayed at a Holiday Inn in Brunswick, Georgia, which is on a harbor of the Atlantic Ocean and around twenty minutes by car from the beach on Jekyll Island. To make the most of our day, we headed to Jekyll about nine o'clock in the morning.

We loved the beach. Oh, it was great! Teresa and Michael played in the sand, ran in the water, and made sandcastles. Since Kenneth was only six months old, we made him a tent out of one of my T-shirts. After enjoying a picnic lunch, we were preparing to leave, when I heard a lady hollering out for help. The tide had pulled her and her young son, four or five years old, out to sea.

I immediately swam out, grabbed her son, and pulled him in. Sandra could not swim, but she waded out to her shoulders and took the boy so that I could get his mother. The current was so strong that I would swim three feet and the tide would take me out two. When we finally got to the shore, I was exhausted. I couldn't do anything but lay down on the beach at the edge of the water.

The crazy thing about the situation was that other people were on the beach, but nobody would swim out to help. I had to make two trips out in the ocean, nearly drowning myself, while others were just standing there, watching like nothing important was taking place. After the fact, some did come up to ask what had happened and expressed gratitude for what we'd done. The mother and son didn't have any friends or family on the beach, so maybe all the others were so involved in what they were doing that they didn't see it as an emergency. Some people need sirens and lights before they realize a crisis is happening.

From spending so much time on the beach, we all got sunburned—all except Kenneth. He was protected under the T-shirt. That evening, as we sat in the restaurant, our teeth began to chatter. Our waitress took one look at us and said, "You better get some Solarcaine!" Thanks to her, we learned about a great remedy for sunburn.

At Home in Myrtle Beach, SC

The next year we went to Myrtle Beach because the tide was not as strong there and the beach had lifeguards. Always frugal, saving for vacations and never overspending, we would stay at the Quality Inn. We never credit-carded our vacations. Our family loved Myrtle Beach so much that after the third year, we bought a timeshare that we owned about fifteen years. The arrangement meant that we "owned" the condo certain weeks of the year.

We were vacationing at Myrtle Beach in 1975, when the movie *Jaws* came out, so Sandra and I thought it would be fun to take the children to see the blockbuster. We didn't realize how scary it would be for adults, much less little kids. Theresa and Michael were rather young, eight and nine, for such a thriller, and Kenneth was only six. No wonder they thought Jaws was in the water and wouldn't go in the ocean the next day! Doing my best to show them they didn't have to worry, I waded in until the water was about two feet deep, but I was as scared as they were. Even in the shallows, the Atlantic Ocean was too dark for me to see my feet or any big fish that might be swimming towards me.

It's a good thing our condo had a pool. We all agreed to spend the day there, where we could see to the bottom.

Over several years, we also went deep sea fishing. It's expensive to charter a boat with a captain, and being frugal, I would think of the dollars and cents. To make our trips worthwhile, we'd always catch plenty to stock our freezer. I found a great captain who knew the best spots for fishing, and we'd catch enough red snapper to feed our family for a year.

Now that I take trips to Florida, I catch redfish and trout with my grandchildren. We have a great time, and I'm teaching them to be frugal. They also set out to catch enough to stock the freezer and feed their family for the whole year.

I've never been against splurging if we could afford the cost. When our family went to Myrtle Beach, we would often go out at midnight for donuts. That's when Krispy Kreme would start frying up fresh batches and notifying the public by lighting up the "Hot Now" on the sign out front. (I'm a big believer in grabbing an opportunity when it's hot.) We'd buy four or five dozen and eat two or three dozen immediately—in the middle of the night!

Our First Night on Walnut Mountain

We didn't need many fancy items or amusements to keep us happy, and we loved being out in nature. During our first visit to Ellijay, Georgia, we decided to buy a lot on Walnut

Mountain and build a cabin later. The place was so pretty, and I was always one to make decisions by instinct. The first night we spent on the mountain reminded me that good instincts included common sense.

In the 1970s, Sears had a big store on Ponce de Leon Avenue in Atlanta. Now renovated, the old building and surrounding area are home to a popular living, shopping and entertainment district called Ponce City Market. Back then, the department store sold a little bit of everything, so while we were there shopping, the kids saw some sporting equipment and began talking about camping out at Ellijay. They wanted me to buy the supplies we'd need, but Sandra reminded me that my buddy Don had some camping equipment. It was her idea to borrow the tents and sleeping bags from him to see how well we liked it.

I did just what Sandra suggested. I loaded up the first new pickup truck I'd bought for Metro Waterproofing with the supplies from Don, food, and other comforts from home, and we headed off to Walnut Mountain.

We chose a spot beside a creek. My being an old soldier and tent specialist, I showed the boys how they could pitch a tent on a high spot near the creek, dig a little moat around the perimeter, and bank the sides so water couldn't come in. We loved it out there, picnicking and telling ghost stories around the fire. About ten o'clock, it started raining, so that was our signal for Sandra and me to put out the campfire and send everyone off to bed.

Since we had air mattresses and sleeping bags, all was perfect until two in the morning. Little Kenneth, five years old, woke us up, saying, "Dad, water." I thought maybe the rain had him worried, so I said, "Boy, you are not getting any water in your tent. It's 2:00 a.m. Go back to sleep." It wasn't long before Michael, who was six and a half, also said there was water in his tent. Just to check, I laid my hand on the ground by the air mattress. We were already surrounded by one and a half inches of water and more was coming inside.

We took down the tent, loaded everything back on the truck, and went all the way home to Lawrenceville. It took me an entire week to get all the mud and sand out of my new truck and to clean the camping equipment and return it to my buddy Don in the proper condition. Ms. Sandra said she didn't want any more camping, so it was on to the luxury life. The next week, upon seeing the model cabin designed to inspire people to build on Walnut Mountain, we bought the model and moved in!

Motorcycles

Sandra and I did not deny our family, or one another, a few special toys. About 1973, when I started making money, I decided I wanted a motorcycle—a toy—so I bought a 350 Kawasaki, new. Kawasaki is a great motorcycle. Oh, how it hums, and that's why dogs like to chase it! After hitting a couple of dogs and nearly getting me killed (Sandra, too, when she was riding with me), I traded it in for a Honda CB500. I loved that bike, but it's human nature to want something bigger and better. I traded up to a Honda CB750.

One fine day in 1975, Sandra and I were out riding at our farm in Statham, Georgia, when we came by the Honda motorcycle shop. By that time, I was a motorcycle nut. We went inside, and Sandra purchased me a brand new, straight drive Honda Gold Wing GL 1000. Candy-apple red, it was my dream. Back then, you could get only fairings (the shells placed over the motorcycle to reduce drag) and luggage racks in black or white. With my perfectionist mind, I would not accept putting a black or white fairing or luggage rack on a candy apple red motorcycle.

To get exactly what I wanted, we had those parts primed in Japan, painted in California, and assembled in Winder, Georgia. My bike became the first dressed-out motorcycle that the Honda dealer had ever seen. Honda International was so impressed with the final product that they took pictures and even considered putting a photograph of my motorcycle and me on the cover of their sales magazine. I did look pretty good in my Johnny Carson suit and motorcycle boots!

I kept the bike for about six years and then started building dune buggies because I liked having a different challenge. A buddy of mine who worked for General Motors helped me, and we built some of the greatest dune buggies that Lawrenceville, Georgia, had ever seen. We would fill some coolers with food and drinks, and drive them to Walnut Mountain. They were traffic-stoppers. One had a candy-apple-red-and-white striped top and the other was black. Both had Model T bodies, no seatbelts, and open-window air conditioning! We put the luxury in the seats, which were made of Lincoln Continental velour, along with installing an AM/FM stereo and a CB radio.

As hard as I worked, I found a few ways to cut loose!

78 One Stop

After Sandra's daddy passed away with cancer, her mother needed something to do. Therefore, in 1976, I bought a convenience store on Highway 78 to help my mother-in-law *and* make an investment. The 78 One Stop was a good little store. We sold gas, and inside, we had a bait shop, as well as sold chicken and biscuits. Grandma (Sandra's mom) made the best biscuits.

One of our most loyal biscuit customers was Phil Niekro, a former Major League Baseball player and one of the Atlanta Braves' greatest pitchers. In 1997, he was inducted in the Baseball Hall of Fame. Since he lived out by our store on 78, Phil would stop for Grandma's biscuits every morning when he was in town. To this day, he says her biscuits were the best and she was the sweetest lady.

Besides giving my mother-in-law something to do and a way to earn some money, the store was a big help to Metro Waterproofing when our country faced a gas shortage. During that time, stations were limiting how much gas people could buy. Some would let you have only three dollars' worth at a time. With the One Stop, we could fill up our truck and go about our business.

Having the store also taught me a lot about that type of retail operation. When you hire people to work in a convenience store, you'll say, "I will give you ten dollars per hour." Your employees are thinking, *I will take ten dollars per hour.* By the time that they help themselves to free drinks, free smokes, and free gas, they end up with twenty dollars an hour: ten in merchandise plus the ten you pay. So, after five years, I sold 78 One Stop in 1981.

The first guy I sold the business to had been a buyer for Rich's Department Store. He was great businessman, but he got into the bookie profession. He'd take bets on football and baseball, and transport people to the games. He'd supply the beer, too. One week, the odds were not in his favor. Paying all that he owed on the bets, my guy couldn't afford to keep operating the store because a gasoline retailer doesn't run on extended credit. When the delivery trucks come with 10,000 gallons of gas, you have to pay the bill. I had financed the sale of the business, so he simply returned the store to me after just one year.

The second gentleman who bought the business had retired from a county job. He was completely lost on how to run the store. For one thing, thinking he'd earn a better profit, he upped the gas prices. Within sixty days he was doing fifty percent of the sales that we had. After three months, he wanted to cut his losses. For me to buy him out, he gave me all the cash he had plus a Gold Spoke Harley Davidson motorcycle. (It would be my last motorcycle.) Between what he'd paid me and what I could have earned had I not sold the store to him, I lost money. I'd had enough! I boarded up the building and started riding the Gold Spoke Harley to endure my loss.

Harry was the third and final gentleman to buy 78 One Stop. He had come to me three times wanting to purchase the store, but I'd refused. I didn't want to finance another sale. But Harry was persistent. A Korean immigrant, he'd been in U.S.A. nine years. He had learned to speak English and saved $100,000. All of that impressed me, so after the third meeting, I decided to sell the store to Harry.

I didn't think he'd ever get the place open because he took so long remodeling. For one thing, he cut the size of the store. I shouldn't have doubted him. From the grand opening on, Harry and his wife ran the business together every day from 7:00 in the morning to 11:00 at night. On top of that, he paid me. If I didn't stop by to get the check on the day it was due, he would hand carry it to me in Scottdale to my office.

After about five years, Harry's wife passed away while standing at the cash register. She'd suffered a heart attack. He sold the property and paid me in full. It was an honor to know Harry.

Helping Fellow Americans

Immigration: Americans Helping Americans

Up to the early 1900s, when immigrants first arrived in America, their primary goal starting out was to obtain their citizenship. They all wanted to become Americans. They risked everything to live in the Land of Opportunity, where they would be free. They understood the cost of freedom; they appreciated that freedom came from working and fighting for it.

More recently, many have gotten the idea that by coming to America, they'll get free handouts. Not all, but many enter the United States with that mindset. They don't place a priority on learning the language and becoming a citizen. They aren't willing to give their loyalty to one flag.

To succeed here, however, your heart must be here. You have to fall in love with America in the same way that you love your family.

Americans, in turn, must embrace immigrants who arrive in the Land of Opportunity, eager and ready to work for a better life. Many perform the kind of backbreaking labor I did as a child— work that few of our physically strongest, adult citizens today would attempt. Working from dusk to dawn, those who value freedom want nothing more than to be legal citizens. Some have advocates, including their employers and churches, but the path to legalization in America is complicated and lengthy. Thus, the average immigrant who loves the United States and wants nothing more than to contribute to the country as a citizen should have the chance to reach that goal through thoughtful, humane and simple solutions.

My plan begins with an executive order that requires all illegal immigrants to visit their local police station or sheriff's office under their jurisdiction. There they would receive a social security card, visa papers and a path to citizenship with a five-year plan that stipulates a series of requirements. The simple process would require administrative personnel to enter the individual's basic information—name, age and address—into a basic form and then submit it online to the Department of Naturalization and Immigration.

All applying must learn English and arrange for their family members to adopt the language. They must take an oath to honor one flag, the flag of the United States of America.

Those who had a misdemeanor crime on record would be eligible for the same five-year visa as all other immigrants. Individuals who had a nonviolent felony crime on their record—i.e., a DUI, domestic problems or minor drug offenses—would be required to work through the judicial system and serve their punishment before they could continue their path to citizenship.

To ensure the safety of American citizens, the United States of America would work with its neighboring countries of Canada and Mexico to set up real security, including walls where necessary, to stop the flow of illegal people and contraband, particularly drugs. Military units that traditionally conducted special training within a few hundred miles of the border would move personnel to the border and plan their training throughout the year at scheduled intervals.

Now, few of the illegal immigrants who had committed a major felony (seven to eight percent of the illegal immigrant population) would show up at a police station. *When*, not *if*, caught, they would be incarcerated or returned to their country of origin.

The cornerstone of any path to citizenship must be patriotism. Immigrants who become United States citizens, therefore, must be people who love the United States and want to live in freedom. They must have skin in the game to know the meaning of being an American, which is why I've proposed a program of service over a five-year period for all who are twenty-four years old and younger. Service could be completed at any volunteer organization: Habitat for Humanity, food banks, health clinics, homeless shelters, shelters for abused women, or even the National Guard. For that service, they would receive the same buck-private pay of someone starting in the military—in other words, a nominal amount. Upon completing the five-year program, each must pass a civics' test to prove knowledge of history and American values.

Our mission is to turn all who are illegals into taxpayers. Consequently, both illegals and employers who operate with cash agreements must be fined penalties that cost more than it would to have paid their taxes.

If you give the United States of America your heart, mind and soul, then you will have everything. You must pledge allegiance to one flag, embrace citizenship, and get some skin in the game by working to make America great.

God gives us dreams and thoughts, but nothing happens if we give up and don't work on them.

Equality and Freedom

The brown skin my family inherited from our Native American ancestors, deepened by the farmers' tans we acquired from working outdoors, kept us rather isolated from various forms of bigotry that the ignorant inflicted on people for no reason other than color. Despite what teachers might be telling students in classrooms today about the bigotry exhibited by whites in the rural South, North Carolina farmers who couldn't spell *integration* practiced the ideal of living and working together long before the Civil Rights Amendment ended segregation. Our lives on the farm demanded racial interdependence. We grew up colorblind.

Skin tone mattered so little to my family that we essentially adopted James, a young African American, as our brother. I don't remember ever learning the circumstances that brought him to us. I simply recall that he showed up one day and didn't want to leave. Thus, we added on a little room to our house and set one more place at the table. Becoming family, James lived and worked with us all throughout my childhood.

Off the farm, the rules were different. We existed within a system of racial segregation and discrimination known as Jim Crow, which prevailed in the southern and border states from 1877 to the mid-1960s. Never taught to hate, I couldn't understand why no black children went to school with me or why my black friends, as close to me as my family, were expected to use specially designated restrooms and water fountains.

Segregation hurt me the most when I one day realized how it affected William, the son of another sharecropper who rented the farm next to ours. In addition to visiting and socializing, our families often helped one another on our respective farms. We didn't see color. My daddy taught me that every man's blood was red and that each put on his pants in the same way.

Since William was older (he was in his twenties when we were in our early teens) and driving his own car, he kindly shuttled my brothers and me to the picture shows (movies) on Saturday nights. Today, such a fine young man would garner respect, but back then, we poor kids were treated with more consideration, as if we were better people, simply because we were white. William wasn't even allowed to sit with us.

Innocently, upon finding our places in the theater, we'd beg him to stay with us. Of course, my brothers and I had read the signs that sent blacks in one direction and whites in another, but we didn't realize how bigoted and angry people could be over integration. We didn't know that the gentle, peaceful man we admired was leaving us in our seats to avoid conflict. That's why he merely waved goodbye before making his way alone upstairs to the "buzzard's roost," the balcony section that kept the blacks separate from the whites below. At the end of the show, he dutifully waited for us to give my brothers and me a ride back home. Despite the humiliation, week after week, William never refused us a ride or acted as if he didn't want to take us.

In retrospect, I believe William's love for us enabled him to endure the humiliation. Compelled by his compassion and humanity, he took it upon himself to provide some hardworking farm boys their cherished escape. His greatest gift was in teaching us that love transcends such barriers, no matter why or how long they existed.

The demeaning practices that I observed in the town were bad enough. Later, when I entered the military, an American institution that was supposedly free of racial prejudice (widely reported as an exclusively Southern atrocity), I witnessed rampant segregation. Within that sick climate of fear and suspicion, white soldiers never mingled with black soldiers. I was the exception. Ignoring the racial divide, I made friends based on how people acted, not how they looked.

Throughout time, men and women like William, although targeted by evil forces, have used the loving spirit within to overcome such hostilities. Instead of fueling the flame of hatred, they have enlightened others, leading by example. Among the most admired advocates of equal rights and civility, Dr. Martin Luther King not only dreamed of a united, integrated America, but his conscience and sense of duty also compelled him to preach and inspire nonviolent social reform.

Born in Atlanta on January 15, 1929, Dr. King was the grandson of Reverend A. D. Williams, pastor of Ebenezer Baptist Church and a founder of Atlanta's NAACP chapter, as well as the son of Martin Luther King, Sr., who succeeded Williams as Ebenezer's pastor and further became an early civil rights leader. Following in his grandfather and father's footsteps seemed the natural path for him, but Dr. King had his own ideas about religion and reform.

After receiving his doctorate from Boston University in 1955, Dr. King turned down prestigious academic positions to accept the pastorate of Dexter Avenue Baptist Church in Montgomery. In that capacity, he took an oath to guide his congregation in the spirit of the Bible. Given his personal magnetism and gift of captivating audiences when he spoke, Dr. King gained national acclaim as the eloquent, charismatic minister and leading voice of equality for all citizens. His influence spread quickly. In December of 1956, the United States Supreme Court declared Alabama's bus segregation laws unconstitutional. Soon after, with him leading the charge, Dr. King had enlisted other Southern black ministers to form the Southern Christian Leadership Conference (SCLC).

On August 23, 1963, over 250,000 people gathered at the Lincoln Memorial to hear Dr. King deliver his most profound message, historically known the "I Have a Dream Speech." The following lines highlight what Dr. King's ideals of freedom and equality: "When the architects of our republic wrote the magnificent words of the Constitution and the Declaration of Independence, they were signing a promissory note to which every American was to fall heir. This note was a promise that all men, yes, black men as well as white men, would be guaranteed the 'unalienable Rights' of 'Life, Liberty and the pursuit of Happiness.'"

He wanted people to be free in the sense of pursuing the American Dream, the opportunity for success and prosperity through personal initiative and work; to be free to live as equals. Freedom was not about getting everything for free and waiting around to be housed, clothed and fed while others did the work. Those who receive items for free are enslaved to the giver and the lender.

By giving handouts, we've enslaved more people in the United States than ever before in our history.

Teaching to Fish, Not Feed

Sandra and I firmly believe in giving people a hand, not a handout. I could relay many stories about how we've helped families through difficult times to ease their burdens, especially around Thanksgiving and Christmas. We've learned from experience that it doesn't pay to keep writing checks, removing the incentive for individuals to help themselves.

In one case, after praying for a young woman while she was hospitalized for an illness, we gave her family a generous cash gift to assist with bills and buy a car. Sandra and I also joyfully took their fifteen-year-old daughter shopping to make her Christmas bright. The mother didn't have much saved from her job working for Walmart, and her husband, who painted houses, was working only part time so that he could spend hours by her bedside and do chores at home to help her through her recovery.

It didn't take long for us to realize that this mom and wife had become too dependent on her husband's care and our charity. When the time was right, I kindly but firmly pointed out that she was physically capable of going back to Walmart; we would not be writing any more checks. Indeed, she returned to work without any problems, her husband got back to painting full time, and the family is now doing well on their own. They no longer ask for one thing from us.

I can present many, many examples of our not only offering a helping hand when needed, but also of teaching people to fish, not feed. We've hired many young people, for instance, to work at Metro Waterproofing. Quite a few teens in high school have held jobs in our company during the summer, and older students have worked with us while taking college classes. In addition to providing a means to earn an income and establish a solid work ethic, our objective is to foster a dream. We encourage our young employees to earn a degree or certification (locally, we have an open-access, liberal arts college and a technical college) and to put their talents to work in a field for five years or so to learn the ropes before going out and starting their own businesses.

Someone must be making the money every day to pay the bills, although individual responsibilities will and should vary. Certain people are not capable of running businesses, managing others, or owning property. Some don't want to be tied down, which is fine if their expectations are not to receive the same luxuries in life as those who've worked diligently (usually by taking risks and assuming tremendous responsibilities) to achieve goals and purchase a comfortable home.

Shouldering significant responsibility is rarely loads of fun or easy, but the reward can be great.

Marching Onward with Purpose

Committed to ending blind racial hatred in America, Dr. King endured many serious tests of his leadership. Critics accused him of everything under the sun, including having too much pride, but he marched on. He continued his crusade even though he and his allies were threatened, and several of his friends were murdered. He knew his life was in jeopardy, but he refused to give up the cause—his true purpose.

Thanks so much to his inspiration, when Dr. King was assassinated, the mission endured.

Few of us are challenged to martyr ourselves for a mission. Tests of faith, nonetheless, invade us each day. Every choice we make entails weighing a personal desire for well-being, security, ease or whatever makes us feel comfortable versus an internal sense of right and wrong. How often do we shush that voice of conscience to avoid the slightest discomfort?

That still, small voice is what arouses a sense of mission and propels us to pursue a higher calling. When we see ourselves as individuals who have a purpose in life, the purpose becomes our life. Once we take the path, the idea of walking away from that duty, even for one weak moment, is worse than dying.

THE JOY OF GIVING

WHAT INSPIRES PEOPLE TO DO great deeds? Often, big initiatives start small, beginning when one person recognizes a single need and grabs the opportunity to address it. In tackling one issue, a true problem solver finds more to do and does more for the cause. Volunteering, in turn, becomes habit forming. Both the need and the ability to make a difference are highly motivating.

Earlier in my married life, I had been active in the Episcopal Church in Morganton, North Carolina. When we moved to Georgia, transforming Metro Waterproofing from an idea into a multimillion-dollar company consumed my days and nights. Every minute, I was focused on growing and improving the business. Always thinking, I kept a tape recorder in my car and by my bedside to capture any thought while driving or any midnight idea that might cross my mind.

Gradually, encouraged by Sandra, who saw me working constantly, I began to get involved in the hobbies that Theresa, Michael and Kenneth pursued. By taking an active role in the interests of my daughter and sons, I found avenues in which to encourage and guide them and their friends as well. Volunteering as a scoutmaster, I led young boys on more adventures than I could count and imparted practical and moral lessons at every step.

Before long, I had become fully committed to each child's clubs, sports and schools. It all started with Michael. About a week after we signed him up to play Pee Wee baseball, I came home from work to hear Sandra inform me that I would be his coach. I informed her that I'd never played an organized sport in my life. No one else would assume the responsibility, however, so she gave me a baseball coaching book. That's when God showed up.

I got to the field and realized my players were all the leftovers, the boys who had not been chosen by any of the other coaches, who had already selected their teams. My boys, however, had good parents, and together, we went on to assemble a winning team. My strategy was simple: If we didn't let our opponents cross home plate, then they couldn't beat us. I used that strategy for nine years, and we always ended the season in first place. On top of that, most of our boys were picked for All Stars throughout high school.

I ended up spending over a decade and untold hours on the playing fields of the Lawrenceville Athletic Association. Now that my children run the business, they wonder how I had the time to devote to them. I made time and got just as much from experiencing every practice and game as the kids. (If I ever missed one of their events, I had a reason and let them know why.)

For a period, we practiced baseball in a cow pasture, so the boys had to watch their step! I wanted them to enjoy the sport, but also to take our practice seriously rather than treat it as playtime. My teams learned to be focused and disciplined. They learned about responsibilities and consequences. If a child missed a ball he should have caught, I'd instruct him to run a lap to a distant fence post. "You'd better run to the pole," I'd say. They loved me and I loved them, so the children obeyed. Influenced by how he was treated at home, however, one little boy thought he should bypass the penalty because he had a physical disability—one that did *not* prevent him from joining the team.

The eight-year-old child was Kenneth's good friend, and I wanted him to learn an important lesson. He would not overcome challenges or achieve goals in life if he used his handicap as an excuse for not trying. And, yes, he ran to the pole. The roundtrip took him about five minutes, maybe twice as long as any of the other kids would have needed, but the boy was clearly pleased with himself when he completed the lap. The child's mother, however, was not happy. After practice, she gave me a piece of her mind, and I gave her a piece of mine. "I'm not going to teach that boy any differently," I told her.

I continued to influence the child, and he greatly respected me. He ended up entering the military, and eventually landed a position in Washington, DC, related to our country's security. As a grown man, he kept in touch, proudly sharing his accomplishments. If I had pampered him all those years ago, I doubt he would have bothered.

Quitting was not allowed in our family. If our children started an activity, they finished it. If they didn't like a sport or hobby, they didn't have to stick with it forever, but they fulfilled their commitment to the end of the year or season. Sometimes, they just needed a little encouragement.

During Michael's first Pee Wee baseball season, he didn't have a single hit at any time he went to bat. He loved the sport, so I took him to the batting cage. The next season and all through high school, he made the All-Star team.

All three took piano lessons, and Michael, who most loved music, also played the trumpet. Sandra used to tell him he'd be the only football player who'd return to the field at half-time as a band member. While both boys did well on the field, only Michael wanted to be on a college team. I didn't realize that Kenneth had different ideas until the end of his senior year of high school. He had broken his ankle during the last game. The injury was a relief to him, but he expressed that to his girlfriend, not to me, and then he recovered. I thought I was encouraging him when I said he still had a chance for a scholarship, although probably from a smaller school. At that point, he wrote me a long letter to tell me he wanted to study engineering at Clemson University. Happy that he had spoken up, I said, "Boy, you never had to play football. I love you!"

Sandra and I always encouraged the three of them to pursue their passions. Also, if they joined a club, we urged them to take a leadership position.

Passion is essential in any endeavor. Our devotion to our children compelled Sandra and me both to join the P.T.A. Contributing our time and resources, we tackled educational concerns by working with fellow parents, teachers, school administrators and the greater community. Opening my eyes to need in the community, I joined civic organizations like the Jaycees and Gwinnett Chamber of Commerce, which fostered a sense of neighborhood and goodwill.

Although I was not raised to be greedy or selfish, growing up poor instilled a strong survival instinct. My entrepreneurial nature also kept me focused on pursuits that fostered my personal well-being and that of my family. Volunteering, however, produced an indescribable satisfaction that comes from helping others out of compassion, love and responsibility, and the seeds of goodwill spread and blossomed. Aside from doing my part as a member of any organization, I found myself being a more caring individual. I was inviting my neighbors for dinner, checking on their homes when they were out of town, and sending meals when they were sick.

The joy of giving became addictive. I didn't require or desire praise. Even so, from volunteering to teach entrepreneurship for Junior Achievement, I was named the 1978-79 Teacher of the Year. Also, my willing leadership in one position placed me in subsequent leadership roles. After Sandra and I helped establish a new Episcopal Church, I was elected senior warden and sat on the Diocesan Council. Truthfully, I served as junior or senior warden so many years since 1969 that I've lost track of how many.

I never volunteered with an expectation of receiving thanks from individuals or institutions. Besides, no reward was ever greater than the personal gratification I felt within.

A Prized Corvette's True Value

It's human nature to dream about having certain material luxuries, and there's no sin in enjoying the fruits of your labor. From my childhood experiences, a Cadillac represented success, but the Corvette was the ultimate dream car. Back in the 1950s, only the wealthy and their kids drove Corvettes. I had a goal to own one, and having a best buddy in the military who possessed such a beauty gave me a greater incentive.

By the time I had enough money, however, I was making sure my three kids each had what I'd lacked as a child. Besides good-quality clothes, I bought nice cars for them. Providing for them derailed my goal until 1992, when I happened to notice a 1978 25th Anniversary Edition Corvette while traveling through Eufaula, Alabama. The owner and I almost got into a fight during the negotiation. He wanted me to buy the car and I wanted to steal it!

We parted ways until the fellow called a few months later to ask if I still wanted to deal. He agreed on my price but asked for payment in hundred-dollar bills. Ha! Concerned for my safety when I withdrew the money from my bank, the security guard escorted me to my car. From there, I drove straight to Eufaula. Once the car was mine, I had the Corvette completely restored. What an unbelievably beautiful car! I can't count how many people wanted to buy it.

No matter how much I loved her, I wasn't married to that car. When one of the interested buyers, a Corvette dealer near my home, was willing to trade my '78 for his new 1994 Corvette Convertible, I jumped on the deal. Of course, I paid him for the difference in value—$10,000 in cash. Not for one minute did I take for granted that I could purchase what was then my dream car by paying cash. My gratitude persisted as I continued to upgrade to the latest model until 2000. That's when Sandra and I were committed to building homes for Habitat for Humanity and I was serving on the organization's board.

The Value of a Home

Millard Fuller and his wife Linda founded Habitat for Humanity. Growing up dirt-poor in rural Alabama, Millard knew the feeling of owning next to nothing, and that emptiness ignited a fire in him to succeed. By working full time, he put himself through Auburn University, and while still at the Tuscaloosa School of Law earning his second degree, he began a marketing firm. By twenty-nine years of age, Milliard was a millionaire.

As time went on, with Millard putting his firm above all else, he had more material riches that he'd ever imagined possible, but at what cost? Was he willing to sacrifice his health (he suffered with severe stomach ulcers) and his marriage for an affluent lifestyle? Realizing that their wealth was ruining all that really mattered to them, Millard and Linda rededicated their lives to serving others. They sold everything and gave away almost every penny.

Following three years of missionary work in Africa, the Fullers returned with a vision to begin a grassroots organization that would provide decent, affordable housing for individuals and families in need. They launched Habitat for Humanity in 1976. Without any government assistance, operating in the United States plus seventy other countries, the nonprofit not only builds homes, but also restores human dignity and fosters self-reliance. Recipients of homes make a deep commitment that includes taking part in the construction process and keeping up their housing payments.

Aware of the impact that a home has on a family and their community for generations, each day, as I walked to my office above the garage where I parked the car, I would hear The Holy Spirit speak to me: *Someone could live in that car.*

God wanted me to give away my dream car.

My kids knew how much I loved the Corvette (like a pretty baby!), so when I told them I planned to sell it and come away with enough money to build two houses for needy families that year, they said, "Don't, Dad, you'll miss the Corvette." I responded that it was only a thing. I could do without it.

Accordingly, I sold the car. During the dedication ceremony of a Habitat home in Centerville, Georgia, I relayed the story of how I'd grown up born poor, worked and attained success, bought something I'd dreamed of owning since childhood, and ended up with much greater joy from using the money to make a significant difference in people's lives. That meant more to me than keeping a fancy car parked in a garage.

In 2007, my son Kenneth, by then president of our corporation, casually asked if Sandra and I had plans for a Thursday evening. We didn't, so arranged to meet with him and the rest of the family at a favorite steakhouse. Once there, they had a surprise gift for me: a 2007 Ron Fellows Edition Corvette Convertible. What a blessing! Working through my children, God not only gave me the gift of a car, but also grateful, loving children who joined together to honor their father. They honor me even more by being loving, giving humanitarians.

As Jesus said to his disciples, "Very truly I tell you, whoever believes in me will do the works I have been doing, and they will do even greater things than these, because I am going to the Father. And I will do whatever you ask in my name, so that the Father may be glorified in the Son." John 14:12-14

When you give everything, He returns the blessings to you—hundredfold.

The Power of Faith

Poverty was the sharecropper's persecution. It separated them from their wealthier neighbors and led to such frustration and despair that the poorest often failed to see a path to a different kind of life: one without misery. Many escaped their hard lives through alcohol. My own father operated a distillery, commonly known as a *still*, that produced moonshine—a drug that produced a little carefree joy and a temporary escape from the day's drudgery. Making moonshine, though, was illegal.

Aside from product safety concerns (the toxic methyl alcohol sometimes found in moonshine can cause blindness and even death), the federal government frowned on home-based businesses like ours that ran on cash. We certainly didn't collect sales taxes or report our revenue. For those reasons, the tax agents, long referred to as *revenuers*, were always looking to shut us down.

To avoid getting caught, Daddy kept his still well hidden by the river. When the time came for my brothers and me to transfer a new batch of moonshine into individual containers, we'd dodge any revenuers who might be searching for little criminals like us by taking a zigzagging path from the river to the corn crib (the building that stored the unhusked corn). There, we'd pour the five-gallon demijohns (large glass bottles) of liquid that we'd carried from the still into smaller mason jars. Finally, we buried the individual jars in the cornfield for safe storage until customers called to buy what they desired of our inventory.

Some would say that my father did no wrong in providing a prized product to his neighbors and earning a little extra cash for his family in return. My mother and the devout members of her church would disagree. They would encourage all the sad folks who invested in those fleeting moments of pleasure to pursue a different path—one that would lead them to eternal bliss.

Eternal Bliss

The Selma Free Will Baptist Church that my mother attended taught me about God. Its traditional roots were as old as America itself, founded as the country was by devout Christians who had suffered persecution in their homelands. As far as she and her congregation were concerned, the Church promised a heavenly reward at the end of a hard life, one that would be glorious and everlasting, in sharp contrast to a few hours of happy drunkenness.

My mother's church, I would realize when older, differed dramatically from the more mainstreamed Protestant Sects. Comprised primarily of the illiterate underclasses, who took a literal interpretation of the Bible and acknowledged a physical relationship with God, the charismatic congregation believed that God spoke to them, watched them, and protected them every minute of their earthly existence.

The Church bestowed dignity, allowing the sharecroppers to endure the backbreaking work at home as well as any public ridicule from those who were better educated and wealthier. More importantly, by ignoring the world's crippling class distinctions, their religion delivered the belief that God's master plan included them right along with the rich bankers, moneyed landowners and well-to-do merchants. Despite whatever the rest of the world denied, Selma Free Will Baptist dispensed courage and self-respect.

Undeniably, my sense of independence and self-worth were always rooted in the rites of this charismatic tradition. No matter how humble, all members sang every word of every hymn at full voice. They made "a joyful noise unto the Lord," Who blessed them in their poverty and ignorance. Even the characteristically rebellious teenagers were moved to face the congregation and testify about the ways of God and how He had worked in their lives. Receiving encouragement to stand up in that manner was the opposite of hearing schoolteachers silence and sentence them to the back rows of classrooms.

Never shy among my own kind, I reveled in the freedom and pleasure of the hymns. The age-old tradition of singing praises and testifying convinced me that I, too, could be a leader; moreover, I would learn, God intended me to be a person who took charge.

"Make a Joyful Noise unto the Lord" – Psalm 98:4

The church left a particularly lasting impression on me when I moved back in with my momma and daddy for a year before joining the military. (In truth, they moved in with me while I helped support them.) While we lived under the same roof, I'd go to church every Friday and Saturday night to sing. Admittedly, the pretty girls went to church, so although my motivations were not all religious, the outcome was great. I didn't know how to read music, but I had a good ear, and I now believe singing was God's way of preparing me for my journey. From singing out, I became a good salesman and leader.

I learned that if you don't sing out, you lose the joy of the hymn. If you don't speak out, you lose the joy of life.

When I was in the military, I continued to love my church experiences, but they were different. We had one service for all denominations—Baptist, Catholic and the others—to learn the Bible and hear the sermon. If we sang, I don't remember our doing so. Something else impressed me: I fell in love in with the quiet and reverence, and in that quiet, I found God.

Later, when I met Sandra, she was attending an Episcopal Church. There, too, the sanctuary was quiet, reminding me of the military churches. The peace gave me time to pray and get to know God before the service. I loved Sandra and the experience, so I chose to become Episcopalian.

The sacred music continued to reassure me that my adopted church offered refuge to all, even a hillbilly like I was at heart. Singing in a choir taught that I was both an individual—a single voice—and a member of a group. In my Episcopal choir, alongside doctors and lawyers, I felt the same sense of interdependence within a community that I'd first known in my mother's rural church. Both choirs also inspired and nurtured the belief that I had something essential to contribute.

Faithful Role Models

Notwithstanding lean years in business, a fire that all but destroyed Metro Waterproofing, two accidents that nearly cost me my life, and illnesses suffered by those dearest to me, I've never doubted my belief. Now a member of the Anglican Church, which reflects my traditional beliefs and values, I continue to live each day of my life with a deepened sense of faith and belonging. Thankful to my mother, who planted the seeds, and my wife Sandra, who cultivated them for over fifty years, I've always known that no matter how dreadful or humble my life became, God Himself had included me in His creation.

Sandra, I must say, set the example of Jesus for me. I have been blessed to have her enter my life. Every day, she has been so patient and kind and understanding, always doing something for others and putting them before herself. She has always put the family first, making sure the children had what they needed, although not necessarily what they wanted. Sandra was the one who brought Jesus into my life—heart and soul—because I watched her live like Him as portrayed in the Bible. Having her as my wife is the greatest honor. Before, when I was far more selfish and gung-ho to make money, buy fancy cars, Sandra remained the stable rock.

Over and over, I have told her how much I love her. Many times, I would call her while I was driving to work or heading back home, and when she'd answer the phone, I'd start singing, "Have I told you lately that I love you?" I could never tell her enough times.

It goes to show you that the individuals you hang around with and the groups you join can influence you to be your greatest or your worse.

Praying for Answers

Shortly after I published an earlier version of *What Can I Do?* in 2000, I gave my heart to God. Before that, I was an acting Christian, going through the motions by attending church and supporting worthy causes, but I didn't truly know God.

People want to know how I'm now different. From my yearning to know God completely and getting to know Him, the simple answer is that I'm kinder, more patient, more understanding and more loving. How did I get to this place in life? For an easy explanation, I can say only that I began to rethink the question of what could I do. Instead, I thought to ask the Lord, "What do *You* want me to do?"

Without hesitation, He called me to help build a church—a familiar mission that would entail assembling committed disciples who'd step forward with financial backing and support the pastor in faith. Sandra and I had previously assisted pastors in establishing two Episcopal churches within our county. This time, however, instead of branching off as we had previously, we were breaking ties.

A group of us had grown uncomfortable with the nontraditional, politically correct path taken by the leadership of our denomination, so a few of us were getting together for Bible study. In our quest to find a church home where we felt we belonged, we created "a place to go" as our motto. During that time, the word spread through Bible study groups that were gathering regularly at restaurants and homes in nearby towns. Sandra and I would often have a crowd of thirty at our house alone.

Suggesting a spiritual leader, one of my friends said, "You need to hear a preacher in Monroe." Apparently, the pastor referenced had not only refused to follow the Diocese of Atlanta's modern views, but in an act of defiance, he had covered the Episcopal signage out front with white paint. I might have been interested in visiting his church if the town of Monroe weren't forty-five minutes away from my home in Lawrenceville. For that reason, I pronounced, "I'm not driving over to Monroe to hear *anyone* speak!"

Despite my words, when Sunday came, Sandra and I found ourselves driving to the church in Monroe. Knowing some of the members, we stayed after the sermon for coffee and cookies, and we spoke with the pastor. The experience was pleasant, but nothing especially compelled us to return. But we did.

On the next Sunday, Sandra and I got in the car with every intention of attending our local church. Funny how *my car* drove us to Monroe! Once again, we stayed for the coffee and cookies, and shook the pastor's hand, but by then we had made up our minds. We were going back to our local church.

An Archbishop Is Born

On Tuesday, nonetheless, Foley Thomas Beach, the pastor in Monroe, called me. "God said you are to be my spiritual mentor," he stated.

"You don't know me from Adam's housecat," I replied, using the old-fashioned expression to say he knew nothing about me.

"I don't," the pastor said, "but God does."

I didn't have an answer; the only way for me to arrive at one was to pray. Giving notice to Sandra, I retreated to the lower level of my home. Some would call it a man cave. It's where I go when I want to pray alone or with others who need prayer. I spent an entire day and a half there before climbing back upstairs to Sandra. (Thankfully, she understands when I need solitude.) "He's got something for me to do," I told her. She knew, of course, that I meant God. That something was to help the pastor in Monroe.

Before he even had a congregation, the pastor was asking me to serve as his senior warden, the head deacon. First on my list was to keep Foley from being defrocked—the same as being fired. The question wasn't *if* the Atlanta Diocese would put a stop to his rebellion, but *when.* Well, an employee isn't fired from a job if the person resigns first, so one of my connections assisted in transferring the pastor's license to the Anglican Diocese of Bolivia. The transfer took place via email and just in time. Indeed, the authorities in Atlanta summoned the disobedient clergyman with the intention of revoking his license, but they were too late.

From the start, we wanted a church that upheld traditional values. Since we were drawing people from several communities, we met in Loganville, a town that was centrally located. (At least it was ten minutes closer to Sandra and me!) Until we had our own building, the cafeteria of Loganville Middle School was home to Holy Cross Anglican Church. On one Saturday afternoon, when we were preparing for a service with anticipation of who would join us at Holy Cross, I leaned on a table set with refreshments to whisper something to Reverend Foley Beach. After, I pulled myself up, unable to hide the pain in my knee.

"Is your leg hurting?" he asked.

"No," I replied. "It's killing me." Hobbling on that bad knee, I already knew from my surgeon that I needed a replacement.

In response, the pastor put his finger on my shoulder. Suddenly, I felt the Holy Spirit descending on me. I can't explain it any other way. I was healed one-hundred percent. I'll never forget the sensation. In the same moment, I was also anointed with the power of holy visions, prophecies and the healing power, as it states in Ephesians 4, which teaches that Christians must be the hands of Christ to do His work. And my life was changed forever.

When you see a miracle and God's hand at work, you are never the same person again: He walks with you and talks with you in everything that you do. John 14:12 says, "Very truly I tell you, whoever believes in me will do the works I have been doing, and they will do even greater things than these, because I am going to the Father." Through faith, an everyday person, just like I am, is an instrument of God, walking in His footsteps and presence all the time.

Just as a note, once we built Holy Cross, forty more Anglican congregations were formed. In just ten years, the Anglican Diocese of the South was also created and Foley was named our first bishop. He went on to become the Archbishop of the Anglican Church in North America. Thinking back to the early days, and considering how we've all been guided, I must say that it's unbelievable what God did.

When you give, He returns the blessing to you.

Praying for Others

I was overjoyed and relieved to have my knee restored, but here's a secret: The one who heals is the one who is blessed. I know this because I've also prayed for others' healing and witnessed those prayers answered. On one occasion, the healing occurred while I was sitting in a pew of our new church, Holy Cross.

Partners in prayer and on the golf course, my friend Walter and I had become close while he'd undergone surgery to remove a cancerous tumor behind his eye—twice. I visited him in the hospital to pray for him during those battles and later when he was diagnosed with lung cancer. Continuing with checkups upon having part of his lung removed, Walter got news that the cancer had returned yet again, showing up in his appendix.

He called me on a Thursday to pray for him. We prayed together over the phone, and I repeated my prayers over the next three days. On Sunday, when he and I were both in church, I heard the Holy Spirit speak to me: *Pray for Walter.* In response, as if casually informing a friend, I pointed my finger and said, "Walter is sitting right in front of me." Of course, he was right there, two pews ahead, so I folded my hands and prayed.

Suddenly, I had a vision of holding his appendix in my hands. It was pearly white, and I knew right then he was cured. His doctor confirmed the good news at Walter's appointment the next day: no more cancer.

Miraculously, my healing prayers have not only continued, but they've also touched the person who means the most to me.

Over the years, Sandra's had her dealings with cancer, including cervical and breast. After undergoing surgeries and treatments for both, she returned to the doctor with dizzy spells. Blood tests indicated that the disease was back, but where? They took biopsies of bone and tissue, but the oncologist couldn't locate the cancer's source.

Dealing with back pain, I don't sleep much more than a few hours each night, so it's not unusual for me to be awake and praying. Deeply concerned for her health, I began praying for her one evening while in bed beside Sandra. "Lay a hand on her head," a voice said to me, and out of nowhere, three angels appeared. They weren't a vision; they were real and humanlike, yet vaporous and ghostly. "Everything's going to be okay," a voice then said, and just like that—*poof*—they were gone!

Immediately, I woke up Sandra and told her, "Your cancer is gone." I relayed what had happened, and we cried and hugged and prayed the rest of the night. At her medical appointment later in the week, the doctor confirmed what the angels had said: her blood tests were clear.

Some have a hard time accepting that miracles happen. I expect people to come up with explanations for my experiences: I wanted to believe God had healed my knee and my mental attitude made it feel better. Walter's cancer-free diagnosis coincidentally came after I had prayed for him. I was dreaming when I saw angels above Sandra. As for her healing, the doctors had never located the cancer, so she probably never had it.

To the doubters, I say, if a miracle happened and you ignored it, the miracle still happened.

One of the most notable miracles of healing I've ever witnessed took place because of sheer faith. On that occasion, I was visiting an assisted living home to lead a Bible study. I had arranged with the activities director, a friend of mine, to meet with the residents in the dining room at lunchtime. (Using the logic that even cows know to come in from the field to eat, I chose a time and place that would draw a good crowd.)

An upscale facility, the place had an elegant dining room with everything beautifully set—white tablecloths, cloth napkins, pretty china, and so forth. I began talking with the activities director and the residents, and all was well until an elderly woman's napkin slid off her lap. When she leaned over to retrieve it, the lady lost her balance, bumping her head against the wall. Simultaneously, her legs got tangled around the chair legs and she fell to the floor.

Following protocol, someone immediately dialed 9-1-1, but I instinctively jumped into action. From serving in the Ambulance Corps while in the military, I was trained to respond as a medic. I ran over to her and untangled her legs and placed a pillow under head. The nurse then arrived by her side, so I got up and started to walk away. That's when I heard the Holy Spirit tell me to go pray for her, so I went back over and kneeled beside her.

She was crying; a goose egg-sized bump had formed on her forehead. It wasn't bleeding, but the bruise was dark red. I looked in her eyes and asked, "Do you believe in God?" She answered, "Yes, I do." Consequently, I asked, "Do you believe He can heal you?" Again, she responded, "Yes." At that point, I put my hand out and said, "Come, Holy Spirit!" With that, she stopped crying and the goose egg vanished within seconds.

The healing didn't happen because I prayed; it occurred because she pronounced her faith in God.

Prayer Followed by Action

Faith and prayer are powerful, but they are often not enough to accomplish tasks that achieve what you need or desire. You must jump into action, and that includes being an example to inspire others. When new employees join Metro Waterproofing, we present opportunities for them to serve God, family, community and country. Besides offering our daily devotionals, our corporate family is so accustomed to taking action that when a need arises, individuals contribute their time and talents like a well-practiced drill.

On an early December morning, for instance, I received a call from a minister who works with the homeless and others who are disadvantaged. He was requesting money to purchase a load of firewood for a family with three small children. Their home furnace had stopped working, and with both parents holding minimum-wage jobs, they couldn't afford the cost of repairs.

When I called my brother to ask if he had any cut logs on hand, my employee overheard me and said, "I have some wood at my house." Another employee asked for the address so that he could haul the load in his truck to the family. Before lunchtime, the wood was stacked in the man's yard at no cost. On top of that, I'd called some friends in the heating and air conditioning business, and they offered to handle the repairs for free. Since I was paying, they charged me only their net cost for the parts.

I also spoke with the family over the phone and plainly told the man that he had to earn more income. If that meant working multiple jobs, then he needed to gain extra employment. We were all pleased to assist him, but I assigned him the responsibility of keeping his family warm, fed and clothed. In fact, I told him if he fit in and had a car, we'd attempt to find him a job at Metro Waterproofing. My offer raised a fundamental issue: his car was not working.

A car in good operating order, I told him, would create opportunity for him. People can get by in Atlanta without a vehicle if they're wealthy enough to hire a car service or they live and work where the public transportation system runs.

His suburban home was not located near a bus route or train, so a vehicle needed to be his priority. It would allow him to double his salary in one week with steady employment and overtime.

His predicament stayed on my mind, and I told the story about the family needing a car at my Christian Brotherhood meeting on Saturday morning of the same week. A fellow in the tire business had the answer. A customer had left a car at his shop with no means or intention to claim it. Just like that, I received the opportunity to purchase a vehicle for $1,400. In addition to giving the man and his family the car, I gave him gas money for the week.

A few weeks later, the man we'd helped called me on the phone just to thank me. He wanted me to know that he and his family were doing well. No longer hobbling along, the father and husband had started his own service business and turned his life around for the better.

I bought a car after working only two weeks for Mr. Hardee at sixteen years of age, and as soon as I left the military, I spent $595, which was every dollar I had, on a 1954 Pontiac. It was like brand new. On top of that, I was a stickler for taking care of my vehicles. Sandra's father taught me that an old car would run thousands (maybe hundreds of thousands) of extra miles if we traveled sixty-five miles per hour rather than eighty, as well as kept the oil changed and the tires aligned.

After a couple of months of driving the Pontiac, I traded it for a 1961 Ford Falcon. The main reason was gas mileage. The Pontiac got only six or seven miles per gallon of gas, while the Falcon ran thirty miles.

Just one year old, the Falcon was bright red with red seats. In addition to saving money because it was less expensive to drive, I loved everything about it, down to the little white buttons on the dashboard that made the interior pop. In return, I sure took care of my prized possession. The shine was so pretty from my weekly waxes that people were scared to touch it. Also, since I was driving that car when Sandra and I married, the Falcon was my good-luck charm.

Remembering how I bought one of my favorite cars on the money I saved in gas alone, I always advise people to calculate their gas and maintenance costs. An affordable vehicle might also make them happier than they ever imagined.

From keeping ambulances in good working order during my military service, I also learned to take care of my cars and be prepared for mechanical problems by having tools and equipment on hand for regular maintenance and emergency repairs. Another lesson came from that experience: as when shopping for the right vehicle, choosing the cheapest part is usually not the wisest option.

When working for Mr. Holbrook, for example, we thought we were saving money by purchasing cheap, used tires. Fully aware that they would not last long, I always kept spares handy on the truck—just in case. The need to change a tire so often also reinforced another lesson in life: I had to do something about my situation (replace the blown-out tire) to change the course of events (move along down the road). In time, I also did some research on tires and found an inexpensive brand that we could afford to purchase new. Those new tires would last longer and ended up saving us money and valuable time in the long run by cutting our replacement cost!

My Episcopal Life

Sandra's godmother had gotten her going to the Episcopal Church—Calvary Parish in Tarboro, North Carolina, one of the oldest Episcopal Churches in the state. Since Sandra wouldn't date me unless I went to church with her, out of my love for her, I became an Episcopalian. I always say that we owe everything to the Episcopalian faith. America does as well. The Constitution was written around the Episcopalian faith.

As Sandra and I moved through life, we would go to the Episcopal Church in whichever town we lived at the time. In different ways, we'd become involved. While we were in Morganton, North Carolina, they needed a person to work with the Boy Scouts. The Scout leader would have to pitch tents and tie knots, so being an old soldier, I said. "I'm your man." Sandra and I were newly married, so the encounter with children and Boy Scouts would be my first as an adult. The experience launched a lifelong of volunteering for the organization. Every year, I now sponsor the American Values Dinner, an annual event that honors members of the local community who support the Boy Scouts. Being active in a congregation is not only about attending services.

When we moved to Georgia in 1969, you couldn't find an Episcopal Church in the Duluth or Lawrenceville area. Sandra, therefore, contacted St. Phillips, the "Mother Church" of the Diocese of Atlanta, and learned that they were starting a mission in Lawrenceville. We met in offices of *The Gwinnett Daily News*, once a regional paper that was owned and published by Robert Fowler, a man who became a great friend and mentor of mine.

Our group started St. Edward's in Lawrenceville. Bob Fowler gave us the land, and some of us mortgaged our homes to finance the building. At that time, I worked with my hands a lot, so I plastered the interior walls of the sanctuary myself. Our need for an organ also marked the beginning of Clyde's World-Famous Barbeque Sauce. My legendary barbeque chicken would raise money for many organizations, but it all began with a fundraiser for the organ. The occasion also sparked my friendship with Don Ross, and our bond is a wonderful testament to church fellowship, which is so vital to church membership.

It's important to note that Don visited me every one of the seventeen days I was in the hospital with kidney stones while I was doing my best to keep Holbrook Waterproofing of Georgia up and running. He is also the man who gave me cash right after the Metro Waterproofing fire and asked for nothing, and showed not a hint of wondering when I could pay him back.

After introducing ourselves on that first day, Don and I got busy with the preparations. We took cinder blocks, rebar, and hog wire to build a fire pit. The rain came soon after we got the chickens started, but from holding a tarp over that pit to keep everything dry, Don and I got to know one another and became best friends. We also sold every bit of the barbeque and raised $270, enough to buy the organ. In time, we cooked so many chickens that we built a real barbeque pit that still stands today behind St. Edward's.

Several families parted from St. Edward's in 1979 because of a conflict within the church. That's when we started St. Matthew's in Snellville. In the beginning, thirty-seven members met at an office. After, we moved into Centerville Elementary School and then to the Snellville Civic Center while the building was under construction. We bought seven acres on Oak Road, and once again, several of us mortgaged our houses to borrow the money. Over the years, I served as junior and senior warden, and contributed financially.

In 1986, the year of Metro Waterproofing's big fire, I was either a junior or senior warden and serving on the vestry (the leadership team). With Sandra influencing me, she and I were tithing a solid ten percent to the church. When told her I couldn't pay the tithes without borrowing the money, she said, "The God I serve won't let you go to the bank!" I didn't go to the bank, and in one year, we doubled our profit at Metro Waterproofing.

By 1997, we were breaking ground for a children's education center. I was convinced that the contractor was trying to overcharge us. I'd figured up the costs and proposed that we should be paying $380,000, which was $100,000 less than the original bid. Everyone agreed. I hired a small contractor to do the day-to-day building, and personally took charge of mentoring the contractor, overseeing the work, and managing the funding.

When the bills would come into Metro Waterproofing, my controller Sam would ask me what to do with the invoices. I'd tell him to file each one, and then I'd pay the bill. I never sent a bill to the church. The Sandra J. Strickland Education Center was dedicated later in the year. Within nine years, we'd paid off all our debts owed from the fire, and in 2000, I gave my heart to God and became a Christian.

We left St. Matthew's in 2003 because the Episcopal Church decided to veer from the traditional values of The Bible. Despite our differences with the churches we built, they remain special in our hearts. Sandra and I weren't planning to plant a new church when we left St. Matthew's, but that's what we did with Holy Cross. In that commitment, she and I took out another loan, marking our third time to finance a church building. The risk—the loan was for two million dollars—would be small relative to all that we gained in renewing the Anglican Church in America.

Instead of tithing (giving ten percent to charity), Sandra and I have often given seventy percent. Our lives of giving, however, have not been focused on donating money. Most of my life has been about doing. I've always said, put your hands to your plow. So, yes, sometimes the purpose of the work, like cooking barbecue chicken, is to raise money. Sometimes it's leading a committee to set goals and achieve them. Even then, money isn't the ultimate purpose; it's a tool.

I don't give money every day of the week, but I mentor someone every day. My goodness! I've helped straighten out more marriages than I could count.

You don't have to belong to a church to do good deeds, but working within the church will change your life in the most amazing ways. You will never be the same or want to be. However, no matter how much people try to influence you about changing with the times or making allowances for new ways of thinking, it's important to know that we are the ones who must change to reap the rewards in this word and in the world to come. The teachings of the Bible never change for our convenience.

One Nation Under God

I've had nineteen visions so far in life, and as of this moment, eighteen of them have come true to the letter. They include people giving their heart to God and being healed from cancer.

Number eighteen was that of Donald Trump becoming the forty-fifth President of the United States. At the time, I really didn't believe Donald Trump would win the election, but God said He was going to send a person who was so strong and powerful and such a patriot that he would change the world and bring Him (God) back into the forefront. That prophesy was what led me to write my emigration program, "A Common-Sense Solution to Emigration."

The Spirit also spoke to me to put Him first, which inspired me to write "One Nation Under God," a call to action for Christian leaders to stand up for God and stand against tyranny and suppression of faith. Emphasizing the need for a strong leader who would stand up to groups like the ACLU, who want to see our way of life destroyed, I implored them to cast their vote for Donald Trump. Only then, I contended, could we bring true freedom to our country and our world, which will lead us to true peace in our collective hearts. Just as God chose Jerusalem as His place for Solomon to build His Temple, so has God chosen America as His place for freedom and salvation throughout the world. Our Founding Fathers knew this and put Him to be in the center of our morals and principles to guide this country.

I've continued the call to action, which has not ended because of an election victory. Churches—most importantly, their pastors—provide an essential line of communication between the people and Washington, D.C. It's up to pastors across this great nation to persist in speaking the truth about the slow and methodical desecration of Christianity. I challenge them to tell their flocks, to inspire them to profess their faith openly and loudly, and to spur them to action. They must save the Christian faith and all religions. *We* must save our families and country.

We must bring God back to the forefront of America. To bring God back, we must bring back the Ten Commandments. The Book of Ethics teaches beliefs that give us a moral compass sent down from God. Ethics guide us to know right from wrong. Nothing in history has established more than the principles of living a just and moral life than the Ten Commandments.

Every time the Ten Commandments are removed from our public places, from our government buildings or from our schools, another thread of the moral fiber that bonds our society and our families is torn. We must bring the Ten Commandments, the Constitution with the Bill of Rights, and the Declaration of Independence—this is what God wants—back to the courthouses, the schoolhouses, the statehouses and the church houses. We must teach them to our children and to the people of our country.

My first eighteen visions have surprised and inspired me as much as they've shocked and encouraged others. Having said that, I can tell you that number nineteen is bigger and greater than all the other visions combined, even as great as they are. It's a vision of crowds walking through the streets, declaring their faith and holding signs that read *One Nation Under God*. It's my belief that we, as Christians, will stop traffic by showing the faith and love He has given us, not by destroying buildings or killing people.

The Bible's Place in Schools

Do you know that the Bible was the first book ever taught in public schools?

Most people who argue against Bible learning in school on the grounds of "separation of church and state" don't know the facts: One, those words do not appear in the Constitution, although the First Amendment is based on the individual's God-given right to practice any religion freely. Two, the Baptists of Virginia were the first to make this an issue by challenging the State of Virginia for establishing an official religion—the Anglican faith—and requiring all citizens to pay taxes to that church. Showing favoritism for one religion made other religions seem illegitimate. Three, their protest in Virginia inspired two Founding Fathers, Thomas Jefferson and James Madison, to support the Baptists' cause. Four, on January 1, 1802, Thomas Jefferson wrote about "a wall of separation between church and state" in a letter to the Danbury, Connecticut Baptist Association, and the sentiments he expressed have been used to interpret the First Amendment's reference to religion.

The First Amendment to the Constitution, which passed on December 15, 1792, reads as follows:

"Congress shall make no law respecting an establishment of religion, or prohibiting the free exercise thereof; or abridging the freedom of speech, or of the press; or the right of the people peaceably to assemble, and to petition the government for a redress of grievances."

Plainly, the government can't tell people what to believe or keep them from exercising their religious beliefs. In fact, to celebrate the First Amendment on the day after it passed, Congress proclaimed a national day of observance. An official National Day of Prayer, which still stands, became law in 1952.

By taking God out of school, we take good out of the hearts and minds of children. Not so long ago, children learned about faith and values at home and at school. Almost all could recite The Ten Commandments. They understood that the Bible was their moral compass to guide them through life. Today, fewer than half of the children in the United States have a father and mother at home to share the responsibility of raising them and drawing the line between right from wrong. For that reason, when I advise teens and young adults, I start with the basics, beginning with the first line of the first Psalm: "The praises of a man are that he did not follow the counsel of the wicked, neither did he stand in the way of sinners nor sit in the company of scorners."

In other words, we all must learn to choose our friends and associates carefully. Far too many teens and young adults get into trouble by allowing people to influence them to do wrong.

For many years, I've visited schools to mentor students. Each child and group is important to me, but I do have a special place in my heart for the young men on our local high school's football team. In turn, they love me, but not because I built a beautiful facility for them with meeting rooms and a first-class weight room. They look me in the eyes and shake hands, fist bump and hug me because they know I want the best for them long after they graduate.

When I meet with them, you can bet I have my Bible with me as my guide to instruct them. I speak to them like I do to my own children and grandchildren. I come right out and tell the team what I expect of them: Don't have premarital sex—no quickies, no five minutes of pleasure. No drugging, no drinking, no bad grades. Don't use bad language. If you do what's right, your life will be good.

I also strive to help them see that not one of us needs a mentor to tell us what's right. We're born with the answers. It's simple: God put this little bell of right and wrong in our hearts. Every time we start to do something wrong, the bell will say, "Don't do that!" When we don't listen, that's when we get into trouble. We don't need a cop waiting on the side of the road to keep us from exceeding the speed limit. We have that little bell.

The longer they're around me, the more times they'll hear me repeat another fundamental message: Doing right doesn't mean that life will be perfect, but leading a principled life matters. Honor and respect matter.

One of the ways I show the football players that I respect them is by wearing their team's colors when meeting with them. Dressed in black from head to toe, I make sure they understand the reason why. "I respect each of you," I say, as opposed to telling them that I'm *proud. Respect* is about them, not me.

Earning respect by accepting responsibility is also among my lessons. As I've pointed out to the young men on the football team, walking around with our heads held high when we've done well is easy. Facing up to those who care for us—parents, bosses, spouses—after doing wrong or failing to succeed is hard. Nevertheless, that's when we most need to look in the eyes of our loved ones and take responsibility. The failure itself doesn't define who we are, but how we handle it says everything.

I've had to reinforce that message many times. On one occasion, for instance, only one of fourteen football players followed through in a commitment to volunteer for a Women's Club event on a Saturday morning. The team had just suffered a devastating Friday night game defeat, and the guys didn't want to face their coach or me. Even worse, they thought, would be the shame of encountering the members of the Women's Club, a loving and devoted group of benefactors.

A few days later at their practice, I assisted the fellows in recognizing the price they'd paid for hiding out: a loss of respect. For over four decades, the Women's Club had supported their high school and their sports team. By letting them down, the fellows had managed to disappoint people who had never failed them. Such behavior was far more shameful than losing a game.

Fruit from the Labor of Others

Every public school in Gwinnett County, Georgia, has a mentoring program that relies on volunteers in the community to spend one-on-one time with troubled students. Some of the boys and girls struggle with grades; others have social problems, such as getting along with their peers. Whatever their issues, those who receive special attention from caring adults graduate high school at a rate that exceeds ninety percent. Therefore, I'm personally involved in recruiting solid individuals to fill the need, and for a time, I was mentoring two boys in middle school.

Each time I'd meet with one of the boys, he'd have an energy bar or two to eat. I remarked that I never bought such expensive snacks when I went to the grocery store. Why, then, wasn't he concerned about the cost? The child replied that he received them free from the cafeteria.

"Do your momma and daddy work?" I asked. He told me, yes, his father was a truck driver and his mother was a nurse for the county prison. "They have good-paying jobs," I pointed out, "but you are allowing the government to pay for your snack." He informed me that the school encouraged him to take advantage of the free food. I emphasized that the food was not free, and no matter what people gave him, he would one day be required to stand on his own two feet.

I doubt I stopped the boy from taking the energy bars that the school pushed on him, but he respected my views and stopped eating them in front of me. Of the many lessons I imparted, that one, I hope, sticks with him the most.

My Passion to Motivate

American Made Movie

In 2010, the Gwinnett Chamber of Commerce honored Sandra and me as Citizens of the Year, giving local media a reason to run stories about us. *Gwinnett Magazine* assigned writer Nathan McGill to our feature, so Sandra and I met with him at our home for an interview. Most of our conversation surrounded tithing and fundraising for the Hope Clinic, an internal medicine clinic in Lawrenceville that operates as a Christian nonprofit for people who have limited access to quality healthcare. Recognizing that we shared similar values, Nathan and I talked about the idea of "made in America."

Soon after that meeting, I had a vision. For years, I had been praying about how to save America from self-destruction. Different ideas had come to me, but during a typical night of minimal sleep, an unusual image materialized on the bedroom wall: a large television screen with a message, *MAKE THIS MOVIE.*

I was used to making things happen, but when I told Sandra, "You won't believe the vision I had," I didn't have any concept of how to make a motivational film. Just as doubtful, my wife responded by saying, "I'd believe anything you told me, but we can't make a movie. We can't even program our iPhones!"

I went about researching what had made America great, and it all began with manufacturing. America led the way in manufacturing, thanks to dreamers and inventors like Henry Ford, who founded the Ford Motor Company. He automated car manufacturing, making the automobile affordable to the working class, by designing an assembly line for the Model T's production. America has thrived on ingenuity and the innovations that put people to work.

Nathan, meanwhile, had produced films and documentaries with his partner Vincent Vittoria through their company, Life Is My Movie. Without realizing it, I'd also planted a seed in Nathan's brain when our conversation had turned to a side topic about manufacturing in America. Taking that idea to the next level, Nathan wrote a film treatment, or the first draft for screenplay, which he shared with Vincent. Vincent liked the idea, but they didn't have money to produce a project of its scope.

Since I had impressed Nathan with my talent for raising money for nonprofits, he asked if I'd meet with him to talk about attracting sponsors. He did not know that I was a philanthropist (I didn't even know I was one until someone defined the word for me) or that I'd have any interest in investing in his project. He just thought that I'd spark ideas about obtaining financial backing.

Sandra and I decided to invite Nathan, Vincent, and both of their wives to our home so that we could get to know them better. Among the questions that we asked was how much money and time were needed to turn the idea into a movie, ready for theaters. If I put up half of the money, the estimate was five to six years. I couldn't let the project take that long; America needed saving right away!

With all parties committed, Sandra and I decided to invest the entire amount. We officially became the executive producers in 2011. The production process, including a good bit of travel to interview and film, began right away and continued into 2012. With the editing of the movie completed in 2013, we premiered *American Made Movie* that same year across the country in a thirty-two-city tour.

As of this writing, over nine hundred schools in the State of Georgia have copies of a curriculum created as an educational supplement to the *American Made Movie.* The purpose is to engage students and others, including employers, about supporting U.S.-based manufacturers. The film is also available to rent or purchase in multiple formats from different sources, including iTunes and Amazon. The Made in America Store, founded by Mark Andol, also retails the movie online and in stores, and distributes the *American Made Movie* to other retailers, like Kinney Drugs, located throughout New York and Vermont.

Our objective for the production was to make an impact. Politically diverse news sources, such as Fox, Huffington Post, ABC World News, and MSNBC, have all run segments about the movie and reached millions of viewers in the U.S. and abroad. We know because influencers from countries like Norway and Germany have contacted us about the message of entrepreneurship in the *American Made Movie.* The pride buying in products made at home is not confined to the United States.

We've further connected with our nation's politicians and lobbyists, who had the opportunity to see the movie when screened in the U. S. Capitol. One of the lobbyists represented Walmart. The film left an impression. Soon after, Walmart initiated a multibillion-dollar campaign and commitment to bringing the American-made ideal back to the country and selling those goods.

Discovery High School

My idea to fund the launch of entrepreneurial classes in my community's schools—Discovery High School and Gwinnett Technical College—emerged from my *American Made Movie* project. I recognized from interviewing manufacturers throughout the country that to encourage job growth in the United States, we needed to train our future workforce to meet on-the-job requirements. We Americans, I also realized, had lost our knowledge of what was good for America, and those values had to be reinstituted.

Sadly, we have lost our way. We want to run into a store or go online to buy something we think we need (or want) as quickly as we can so that we can go back to doing what we love or what we believe is more important. In most cases, the material things quickly lose value, not only in terms of what we paid for them, but in what they add to our lives.

While the sharing a message of taking pride in products made at home, *American Made Movie* more emphatically highlighted for me just how oblivious Americans had become to what made America great. Hint: America's greatness has nothing to do with products.

Freedom made America great. Furthermore, employing people and making them self-reliant has far more to do with freedom than economics. Every time that you lose a job and must take a handout from the government, you lose a bit of freedom. Every job, therefore, serves a vital purpose. People love to speak negatively about jobs that pay a minimum wage, but an entry-level position at a fast food restaurant like McDonald's is an important stepping stone to higher paying jobs and a learning experience towards a good career. (Many other terms could be substituted for *fast food restaurant*—grocery store, department store, factory, construction site, etc.)

If you were to initiate the principles of *What Can I Do?* while working in an entry-level position at McDonald's or a similar operation, you could become a manager earning a good salary within a short period. Also, if you stayed on that track, you'd be placed in charge of multiple stores (or operations) and more people, and doing well financially, within a reasonably short timeframe. It's all about how you apply yourself. High-achieving opportunities exist in all industries.

Acquiring the real-life skills that are intended to groom them for business ownership, Lawrenceville, Georgia, high school students from each grade attend a class in entrepreneurship at Discovery High School. From learning the character qualities and preparation necessary to succeed in business, they come up with their own ideas and plans that they pitch to local men and women in business who have the means (and the possible desire) to invest in them. Some students, for instance, operate a printing business, and they design and manufacture customized promotional items that they sell to customers.

I have met many young men and women who are smart and ambitious, but some occasionally lose their focus. Some lack gratitude for the opportunity they've been granted. When they need a reality check, their teacher calls me to provide it for her class. I'll arrive with a topic in mind, but always keep my eyes and ears open for a direction that my talk should take. One morning, upon entering the state-of-the-art building that exists thanks to taxpayers and generous donations from the local community, I read a sign that notified students of the free breakfasts and lunches available to them. I had my topic!

Once in front of the students, I asked them, "Where do you think that money for the meals comes from?" Explaining that nothing was free because the government would eventually collect the money from them when they went to work, I said, "If you have the attitude that you should be given a free breakfast, free lunch or free college, you are not going to be an entrepreneur." An entrepreneur, I informed them, worked eighteen hours every day, climbing out of the hole until the business finally earned more money than it cost to operate it. "If you don't want to be an entrepreneur," I continued, "then go to another class."

One of the easiest ways to lose self-respect is to become complacent or comfortable with the status quo. Complacency—feeling just fine with the way things are and having no ambition to improve your situation or to help make conditions better for others—destroys more relationships than any other condition. It destroys companies, marriages, friendships. It destroys countries.

The class further got a lesson in economics and the trillions of dollars that the United States owed to foreign nations from spending more than what all the taxpayers combined could afford to pay back. Most listened intently and several took pages of notes. (One boy fell asleep. I purposely spoke loudly and he fell out of his chair!) Incredibly, those who were there to learn had no prior knowledge of the national debt—the trillions of dollars they would one day be responsible for repaying. We discussed obligations facing an entrepreneur: to oneself, family, business, community and country—in that order.

Parents, teachers and all others who step up to mentor young people should not be afraid of honesty. We must lay the truth on the table. Children want to know the truth: Life is hard. No one will hand you a house, a car, food. People don't give you this stuff. We have a workforce that produces dollars. All that you have comes from the fruit of your labor. Walk out to the backyard and see if you find a money tree out there.

Life is hard, but every day does not need to be a struggle. Entrepreneurs work hard and they work in ways that are smart to maximize results, pursue new opportunities, and enjoy the fruits of their labor.

Smart about Work

While running Metro Waterproofing, I was always available to my customers and looking for new business. Answering the phone at 1:00 a.m. or 2:00 a.m. was a regular occurrence. My kids didn't like it, but we could be on our way to Myrtle Beach for a vacation when I'd spot a building that needed repair. I'd stop the car, get out my pen and pad, and write up a quote for the job. "Get it while it's hot," I'd say to the family.

Two hands can only do so much. I learned quickly that I could accomplish far more by developing a plan and surrounding myself with a variety of people, each with different skills and interests, to perform all the separate jobs as required. Likewise, I've always trained people as quickly as I could and motivated them to succeed in those tasks so that I could get busy working in another area. I trained my children to take over Metro Waterproofing, and they not only accomplished the jobs they were taught, but they also expanded the business and achieved even more on their own.

Entrepreneurs have a way of taking over. They jump into the driver's seat because they realize that the person behind the wheel is the person in control. However, whether to focus on the next great opportunity or to take a vacation, entrepreneurs achieve what they desire by knowing when to move aside to let others do their jobs. People at the top of every successful organization have checks in place to monitor progress and address problems, but they don't micromanage. They rely on capable managers to succeed on their own.

Good businesspeople further know that they must remain involved at some level and choose managers wisely. In one case, Metro Waterproofing had a multimillion-dollar job in Florida that was on track to lose $250,000. Rather than investigate by phone, I got on a plane and went directly to the site. Once there, I saw with my own eyes that no one was working. The people we'd hired to work were all hanging out at the bar and hotel!

I fired all twenty-five on the spot and hired a fresh crew of day laborers who didn't know the first thing about waterproofing. They were motivated to learn and work. One fellow from Alaska turned out to be a great assistant. I remained in Florida for ten weeks—with a short vacation in the hospital from overexertion—and we ended up earning a profit of $240,000.

All my life, I have had an entrepreneurial spirit, but I had some lessons to learn. Right after Sandra and I married, I would borrow my father-in-law's truck and sell sweet potatoes door-to-door until I could afford to buy my own. On one occasion, I accidentally scraped the side of his brand-new truck. I also made the mistake of replacing the amount of gas I'd used, but didn't fill up the tank. Teaching me respect, Pops told me, "Next time, you fill a tank full when you bring it back." The extra amount was a gesture of gratitude. He never had to repeat that message to me.

From launching several different companies, I've learned that getting a business up and running is not the hard part; what's tough is staying in business. You can't just make money; you must earn a profit. Sandra's dad would call it the *loading money*. If we didn't save the amount to operate plus ten percent, we wouldn't survive.

To continue earning money, I also understood the importance of treating people the way I'd want to be treated and putting my customers first. When new employees joined my company, I'd advise them all to finish every job until the customer was happy. The added cost to Metro Waterproofing and an employee's extra sacrifice didn't matter. If our customers were smiling, then we'd stay in business. People talk. One happy customer would tell a few friends, and when they spread the word, we'd end up with ten more jobs. One unhappy customer, however, would tell everyone.

That's the kind of practical wisdom I like to share with young people. Grateful for my perspectives, students at Discovery High School always wait after class to shake my hand or exchange a hug.

The Man in the Mirror

After considering what we are capable of accomplishing, next comes the doing. Thinking and planning are important, but they are preliminary steps. We need busy minds *and* busy hands, guided by four corner posts: love of God, family, job and country. Keep in mind that those values, which give structure to our lives, coupled with the freedom to think and do for ourselves, have enabled one generation after the next to achieve the American Dream and build the greatest country of our era.

At the end of each day, I face myself in the mirror and ask, *what have you done?* Knowing that I'll put myself to the test, I can't be idle. I couldn't stand to admit to myself that I hadn't done one good thing.

At the start of each day, you must look in the mirror and ask, *what can I do?* Go back, then, at the end of the day to face yourself and ask, *what have I done?*

You're Never Too Old

You are never too old to attempt something new and excel at it if you put your mind to it.

On my sixtieth birthday, my son Michael gave me a used set of golf clubs. I put them in the garage, where they stayed for several months. I'd never played golf and didn't know the difference between a sand wedge and a driver. Finally, I accepted the challenge and went to the driving range. After that first day, my friend Bill Guthrie gave me a Ben Hogan book to help me learn how to improve my golf grip and swing. After practicing a bit, I returned to the driving range. If I were to improve, I needed a pro to teach me the fundamentals.

People assumed I would be old-fashioned about taking instructions from a female, but I didn't mind a bit that a lady named BJ was the pro—if she could hit the ball and teach me to do the same! We began with her presenting a basket of balls and telling me to get out my seven iron. She showed me how to change my grip and told me to hit all the balls in the basket. I was to continue hitting with the same club for six months. With my military background, I was used to accepting regimented orders, so I listened. Day after day, I returned to the driving range, pulled out my seven iron, and hit more balls than I could tell you.

By the end of the first year, I broke one hundred. During the second year, I broke ninety. (For reference, hitting 108 on a par seventy-two course is considered quite good. Many beginners hit in the high 170s.) At the age of seventy-one, I shot my age for the first time.

That same year, when Sandra and I were playing one day, she commented, "You're hitting that ball pretty well." On the last hole, still a distance from the green, I said, "If I can get that ball right there, I'll shoot my age today." Instead of shooting par, or sinking the ball within the exact number of shots designated for the hole, I birdied, meaning I hit one under par. Therefore, instead of shooting a seventy-one for the eighteen holes, I shot a seventy.

My improving golf game earned me a place (multiple years) in the Mitsubishi Pro-Am PGA Tour, allowing me to play with ten incredible professional golfers at different times. I've also enjoyed numerous courses—from Dodge City, Kansas, to the world-famous St. Andrews in Scotland.

I've been a lucky man by changing my fate, not relying on luck!

Count Your Blessings

I'm a blessed man, and every time I count my blessings, I am blessed again for the fact that I have taken a moment to appreciate them and thank God.

For one thing, God gave me the will to overcome every obstacle I faced without my being educated in any formal way.

Whatever came up, I had the will—the wherewithal—to overcome it.

He gave me the greatest gift in Sandra and the blessings of three good children. To this day, our children are God-fearing, tithing, giving and hardworking.

I love showing my adoration and appreciation for Sandra, but she is not a person who craves elaborate gifts. No matter what we could afford, she's always wanted only a little white house with a white picket fence. She never wanted other people to think she had money, so for years she wouldn't drive a car any better than a Chevrolet station wagon. However, in 1988, as a gift for our twenty-first anniversary, I took her to the Cadillac dealership. Without her knowing, I had bought Sandra her first Cadillac, baby blue. She didn't want it at first, but after driving the car, she fell in love with it.

My special surprise nearly gave her a heart attack on our twenty-fifth anniversary. I traded out her original wedding ring with the little diamond that she could barely see with a three-and-a-half-carat diamond ring. She still loves the band with the tiny diamond and wears it, but she cherishes the more valuable ring as an expression of my great love for her.

Oh, What You Can Do with Nothing!

Over twenty years ago, I was manning a barbecue grill to raise money and celebrate a milestone—the first move-in day for families of Rainbow Village, a nonprofit that provides a safe, stable housing community for homeless parents and their children. Parents must demonstrate their commitment to becoming self-sufficient and participate in all the required programs. By receiving education, gaining skills and acquiring jobs to live independently, they end the cycle of poverty, homelessness and domestic violence. During the ribbon-cutting event, I cooked 350 chickens. To be clear, I had an enormous grill, but not a fancy one. I didn't even buy it.

We made the cooker from a twenty-foot drainage pipe, found in a dump. I had the pipe cut in two, making half a cylinder, and we welded six legs on it. We also made a big grate for the grill from steel draining plates. A pickup truck transported the giant, which had to be tied down with ropes. It would hold 121 half-chickens at a time!

For twenty years, that grill traveled to ball fields, churches and other fundraising venues, where people bought barbeque chickens as fast as I could cook them. No store-bought grill has made such tender, succulent chicken. It touched every part of Gwinnett County, doing so much good that people started referring to Clyde's World-Famous Barbeque Sauce as Clyde's Holy Sauce.

People knew I'd pile the food high on their plates, and even if they couldn't eat all their lunch, they'd still buy more chicken to take home for dinner. With all our cooking, we eventually burned too many holes in the bottom of that grill to keep patching it, so I laid my reliable old friend to rest.

I still had plenty of grilling ahead of me, so I drove to North Carolina with payment for a new grill: two Atlanta Falcons' football tickets for a playoff game with the Charlotte Panthers. The seller of the fancy grill, my nephew, took the tickets in trade. The new contraption would also make great chicken, but the main reason people have continued to flock to Chef Clyde has been my sauce.

A church fundraiser proved my point. By giving out $10,000 in total, or one hundred to each adult and ten to each participating child, our objective was to encourage all to use their talents to multiply the good they could achieve. As the senior warden, I felt that I'd done enough participating, so I didn't take one hundred for the challenge. Sandra had different ideas.

About two weeks before we were supposed to turn in our fundraising profits, she asked, "What are you doing with your money?" She went on to insist that I had to help her sell my sauce. I replied that I'd promised Jesus that I'd never sell the sauce because of all the good accomplished with it. But, as Sandra pointed out, we would be selling it to do even more good.

Before I could argue with her, pint jars, vinegar, pepper and the other sauce ingredients, purchased in bulk, cluttered our hallway and garage. Clearly, it was time to grab an apron. Since I didn't have a precise formula, I made my first batch in a two-gallon pot while carefully recording the measurements. We filled 220 jars with Clyde's World Famous Barbeque Sauce and labeled each one.

My job wasn't complete. Sandra instructed me to take all 220 jars to Metro Waterproofing and sell them. I didn't expect to sell one, but they were all bought in the first hour. On top of that, I returned home with an additional 280 orders. We went on to sell another 200 jars at the church. Some, we sold twice, as when a person made a purchase and left it beside me to babysit. I was too busy selling to watch over someone's jars, so if the purchase got sold to another customer, too bad!

In the end, we netted $1,600. It's amazing what you can do with God's grace and a willing mind to go out there and make it work.

Back to Rainbow Village, Sandra and I, among other Gwinnett citizens, like Scott Hudgens, have contributed generous amounts of money to Rainbow Village. More inspiring than our donations, many former residents of Rainbow Village have graduated college, secured good jobs, and returned to give their time and money as others have done before them.

It's been a special walk.

Have a Heart

You never know what opening your heart to others will accomplish.

For many years, Gwinnett County, the largest county in Georgia, did not have a hospital equipped to perform intricate heart surgeries. While other heart-specialty hospitals were not far away, only twenty-five or so miles for the closest residents when traffic was light, a normal rush hour in metropolitan Atlanta would multiply the arrival time by a large factor. The anticipated forty-minute trip could turn into an hour or more on the road. Stuck on the highway in an ambulance going nowhere, people were dying on their way to those facilities.

When Gwinnett Medical Center was seeking approval to build a heart center, John Riddle, who was then the executive director of the Gwinnett Medical Center Foundation, spoke to Sandra and me about the benefits to the community. He not only wanted us to contribute one million dollars, but also to make our donation the lead gift to build community support and demonstrate to the State of Georgia that Gwinnett Medical Center had the talent and commitment to succeed in the initiative. John intended to use us as an example to make an impact. If other potential donors who could afford to give more than $25,000 or $50,000 knew that we had done so, then they would be encouraged to increase their contributions.

From 2007 to 2011, individuals and organizations donated over nine million dollars. In addition, more than one thousand citizens in the community petitioned the State of Georgia in a letter-writing campaign that demonstrated need. A heart center, they said, wasn't just a matter of convenience. Thanks to many joining the cause, the state approved the certification for an open-heart program in 2008.

Up to that point, Sandra and I had made a habit of giving anonymously rather than publicizing our names. That's not to say that we hadn't been honored, but we had never put ourselves forward as figureheads. Praying over the decision, we agreed that leading was important.

I felt that if we could save a life, God could save the soul. In other words, when people are in stress and need, and they are hurting, that's when they are more susceptible to changing their heart and giving their life to God. The vision of that motivated me.

The Strickland Heart Center officially opened in 2012. As of now, Gwinnett Medical Center's state-of-the-art heart facilities and top specialists have saved upwards of eight hundred lives per year. Not many days go by before someone expresses thanks to Sandra or me for the role we've played in saving the individual's life or a loved one's, and we are humbled by those words. It touches me so strongly that Sandra and I, two simple people, can set an example to do such great things.

Whatever we do, of course, we never lose sight of the fact that we are just vessels.

The Strickland Family

Reading was a favorite pastime in the Strickland household.
Theresa, Kenneth, Michael

Back row:
Skooter (Theresa's husband), Erica (Grandchild),Theresa, Sandra, Clyde
Front row:
Dylan, Levi, Chase, Emma, Gabby (Great Grandchildren)

Aaron, Ethan Tyler Ken Teri
Saige Colin Tatum, Strickland

Mike, Bailey & Haley Strickland

Front row: Gabby, Dylan, Emma, Chase
Back Row: Theresa, Skooter, Teresa, Tiffany & Erica
Top shoulders: Levi

Strickland Family Thanksgiving 2017

CLYDE-ISMS FOR SUCCESS IN LIFE

My family, friends and many others I've mentored have a term for my words of wisdom: *Clyde-isms.* Although they like to joke around by imitating how I sound when I give them advice, each one knows I'm right. They can all give you one example after another of how they've succeeded in different ways because they've listened to me.

If you follow every word, you should become a millionaire within ten years. You'll certainly be much happier and more fulfilled in your career and personal life.

Arrive on time.
The first impression you make lasts the longest. Being on time or early shows your employers and managers that you take your responsibility towards them seriously and you respect them. Punctuality is fundamental, but I also say if you're not fifteen minutes early, then you're late. When you're punctual and reliable, you also earn your employer's approval and positive attention. When you're late, you stand out as someone

who doesn't mind causing others—the boss, your coworkers, and people who report to you—to wait for you or to do your work.

With no buses or taxies in our rural area (or money in my pocket to afford such transportation if it had been available), I had to hitch free rides from passersby to my first job off the farm. Consequently, I left the house well before the sun rose to arrive in time to begin preparing food for Mr. Hardee's restaurant. With my first paycheck, I bought a car to ensure I never missed a day or showed up late.

DRESS FOR THE JOB.

Dressing appropriately and neatly assures your employer that you are not only prepared for the work, but you also take pride in the job. It's human nature to form expectations about a person's attitude based upon appearance. Employers will assume that if you're well-groomed, you'll perform well, and if you're sloppy, you'll take a sloppy approach to your job.

When I first started Metro Waterproofing, I didn't have much money to spend on clothes. However, I bought affordable sports jackets from a manufacturer that sold directly to the public. Named the best-dressed contractor in Atlanta, I witnessed the way prospective customers took me seriously. By looking successful, I felt more self-assured. In turn, people were more eager to do business with me because I emitted confidence and seemed capable.

Be the first to volunteer and the last to quit. Volunteering first for a task and seeing the job through to the end impresses an employer by proving your commitment to your company, inspires your fellow workers to step up and do something for the team, and builds personal self-confidence. Such enthusiasm sets a positive example and spreads through a company. Working in a company in which people set out to accomplish great things is not only more pleasant, but also more financially rewarding.

While in the military, I eagerly volunteered. My commanding officers rewarded me with more and more responsibility, and soon placed me in charge of overseeing others who did the physical labor.

Let safety be your first and foremost concern. Every employee depends on a company's success for a paycheck, so each one should be cautious about safety, especially when the work environment is hazardous. Work accidents create such a financial burden that they have ruined many great organizations. I've been an eyewitness to innumerable serious injuries over the years at Metro Waterproofing and two deaths, and all were the result of simple carelessness or not heeding to safety regulations. Aside from destroying a company, negligence, if it doesn't kill you or someone else, can cause extended or lifelong suffering.

Mr. Holbrook was fortunate that I wasn't the type of person to sue him for the fall Leroy caused from his failure to secure the scaffolding.

Earn a slow nickel, not a fast dime.

A quick profit—or fast dime—ends up costing money. First, working in a hasty, disorderly manner compromises safety. Second, hurried work often leads to shabby results that must be repeated, thereby taking twice the labor and time than necessary to accomplish the task correctly. Third, people trust you and your product or service when you reliably produce good quality.

I learned from Mr. Hardee and my father-in-law that a quick sale meant nothing if I didn't earn the loyalty of happy customers. Unhappy customers would tell everyone. Those we pleased would share their positive experiences with a few of their friends and family members, and their referrals were golden.

Work eight hours for eight hours' pay.

If your employer paid you haphazardly, such as by issuing checks for less than you'd earned and by skipping payments, you would demand your money and maybe even file a lawsuit. Your complaint would be legitimate. Similarly, an employer has every reason to expect workers to work a full day for a day's paycheck. Stretching lunch hours, loafing when the manager is away, and using phones, computers and other items for personal reasons all cheat your employer of your time. Those stolen minutes add up and weaken your company.

Noticing that we were losing money on an out-of-state project that should have been profitable, I flew to the jobsite in Florida to investigate the problem. The crew and their foreman lacked ethics and intelligence. I don't know how long they thought they could hang out at the hotel pool and drink beer all day without anyone noticing, but I fired them all on the spot.

Protect company property.

Only two names appear on your paycheck: your employer's and yours. Therefore, that which is in the best interests of your employer should also be in yours. If not, then you need to work for someone else. Protecting company property includes exposing any theft that you witness. Calling people out can be uncomfortable, but if you look the other way, then you cannot complain when your boss says that profits are not strong enough to pay you the raise you were promised or even keep you on the payroll.

I was a kid of sixteen and newly employed when I informed an older cook who was stealing a ham that I'd tell Mr. Hardee. I didn't care if people thought I was a snitch. I was loyal to Mr. Hardee for entrusting me with a job.

Learn the company's policies.

Knowing your employer's rules and their relationship to important goals makes your role in the process more fulfilling to you, as well as more meaningful to your career and your company. Bosses further appreciate an employee like you, who deals with issues more capably and independently by understanding *why*. Your initiative, in turn, separates you from ordinary workers, who do their jobs like robots.

Sam, my loyal controller for thirty years, made sure everyone, even my children, followed company policy. His knowledge and loyalty were invaluable to me and to Metro Waterproofing. Sam saw to it that if we changed a policy, we did so for good reason, not mere convenience.

Learn your job.

Educate yourself. Take classes, read, earn the degrees or certifications to know and perform your job well. Education fortifies your confidence and competence. In addition to gaining satisfaction from your own high performance, you avoid stress from making mistakes or working harder than necessary. You'll likely find ways to work even more efficiently and earn promotions. Also, by taking advantage of educational opportunities, you'll either advance with your current company or move on to a better job with a different employer.

I made up for a lack of formal education by reading. I also enrolled in night classes to become an expert in my field and gain business insights. Sticking to the program required discipline. Besides scheduling night classes after work, I often found the only time to study was while sitting up overnight in the hospital with Theresa, who was there to receive life-or-death asthma treatments. If any person had good excuses to quit, I did, but my efforts presented advantages in business and great rewards.

USE THE FORCE OF PEOPLE AROUND YOU.

Look for the potential in individuals and demonstrate your confidence in what they can do. By delegating responsibility to them, you will enable them to believe in themselves and perform. Also, learn to cooperate. You'll accomplish many times more than what you could do individually.

I've given many young people the opportunity to work and acquire skills at Metro Waterproofing. From their accomplishments, our company has prospered. Many have further started their own companies that enrich our community.

TREAT EVERY PERSON LIKE YOU'D WANT TO BE TREATED.

The foundation of every religion, the principle of treating others the way we want to be treated extends to the workplace. Friendly, compassionate individuals, who are usually the most willing to volunteer, contribute more to a company's culture and often gain the favor of bosses and secure promotions over people who are more brilliant and competent but miserable. Miserable bosses who mistreat their employees also experience high turnover.

Abused by my father one too many times, I left the farm and went to work for Mr. Hardee, who demonstrated the value of treating employees well. He earned our respect, which compelled most of us to make every effort to please our customers.

Sing your company's praises.

You and every other person in your organization should be cheerleading on the same team for the same common goals. Your employment means you have a vested interest in upholding and improving your company's reputation, which is tied to yours. In addition to behaving with integrity, watch your speech. Words have real consequences. Speaking positively about your company leads to positive actions and outcomes. Speaking negatively impacts behavior and destroys reputations.

By singing the praises of Holbrook Waterproofing, I created a great position for Mr. Holbrook in the Atlanta market. At the same time, I established a positive name for myself.

When you reach a plateau, find another hill to climb.

In every job you do, sooner or later, you'll realize you need a fresh challenge. That's when you must expand your vision and talents to climb higher.

Looking for new opportunities to learn, I found plenty to interest me in the waterproofing business. As I continued to explore, I entered the specialty field of historic renovations. Through my expanded interests and education, I amassed valuable skills and knowledge to the benefit of Metro Waterproofing and to others in the industry.

LOVE YOUR JOB OR FIND ANOTHER ONE.

Your heart must be in your work to do your best and succeed.

Either for lack of opportunity or interest, I have left more jobs over a few years than many people have held in a lifetime. I never regretted moving on. Every experience, even the ones that weren't great, taught me something. Hauling dirt in the morning before my factory shift (while my co-workers slept) taught me that working diligently would grant dignity and satisfaction from providing a good income for my family.

EVERY TIME YOU DO SOMETHING, YOU LEARN SOMETHING.

You're supposed to make mistakes, but learn from them. I always say that they put erasers on pencils because when we're looking to solve problems, we're bound to make mistakes.

My brothers and I learned that a little dynamite would blow up several fields of tobacco and blast the glass panes out of every window within earshot. We further realized that by taking responsibility for our actions, we could work to compensate our father and neighbors for the losses they incurred and gain their respect.

LEARN FROM EVERYTHING AROUND YOU.
Never prejudge what a person or situation can or cannot teach you.

In passing my jobsite, an old wino commented that if he were removing caulk, he'd use a jigsaw knife. His remark forever changed our process at Metro Waterproofing and eventually impacted the entire industry.

IF YOU'RE GOING TO CATCH FISH, THEN YOU HAVE TO KEEP YOUR POLE IN THE WATER.
Have a plan and purpose, and stick to it. Don't give up.

I did not allow my start in life on a tobacco farm to become my destiny; instead, my determination not to live that way fueled my motivation to succeed. Whatever it took, I would one day drive my own big, black Cadillac.

IF YOU DON'T WORK, YOU DON'T EAT.
Nothing is free. Even if you get a handout, the meal or bed you receive comes with a price. Taking freebies makes you enslaved to the giver and the lender. When you make others

responsible for your welfare, you lose the freedom to choose what's best for you. This does not apply to the sick or elderly. Also, at times, people need a hand up.

Sandra and I wholeheartedly give our support to individuals, families and programs that focus on lending a helping hand towards self-sufficiency. In one situation, various friends and I pooled our resources to provide heat for a family's home in winter and obtain a vehicle so the head of the household could reliably return to work and earn a consistent income as a self-employed contractor. He later called me to thank me for stepping in. The self-confidence he'd lacked before had returned; I heard it in his voice. Free to pursue his dreams and help his children achieved theirs, the man was happier than ever.

YOU MUST PLAN FOR LEAVING AND FOR CLIMBING THE TREE TO SUCCESS.

Never quit a job unless you have one.

I've always calculated how much income I needed to fulfill the obligations of the day and proceeded to earn that amount plus extra to save for unexpected expenses. Only once did I leave a job without another one waiting for me, but even then, I immediately got to work without any notion that I was too good for a certain type of labor. I left a job with people reporting to me to begin hauling produce. I further took steps to lower our household's requirements, such as by trading my car for a less expensive model that cost less to operate.

BEAT YOUR OWN PATH AND YOUR LIFE WILL BE BRIGHTER.
Don't follow others. Make your own decisions. Learn, plan and work towards goals that put you in control of your destiny.

Realizing that Mr. Holbrook would not honor an agreement over my compensation for building Holbrook Waterproofing of Georgia, I knew the time had come for Sandra and me to launch our own company, Metro Waterproofing. I was never happier than when I ran my own business.

HE WHO TAKES CHARGE WILL BE IN CHARGE.
By taking responsibility, you gain control over the process and outcome. You further get to see for yourself and prove to others what you can do.

I've always let my bosses and my competition know that I was on a path to succeed. If they stayed in one place, they would be left behind as I jumped ahead. My former employers always promoted me quickly unless I left their companies before they had the chance.

IF YOU DON'T SING OUT, YOU LOSE THE JOY OF THE HYMN.
IF YOU DON'T SPEAK OUT, YOU LOSE THE JOY OF LIFE.
Demonstrating your faith in God enables you to gain confidence in yourself.

By singing out in our little country church, I gained enough confidence to speak out as a volunteer in the military. Later, joining a church and choir with congregants who were highly respected professionals in my community, I recognized that I, too, had something worthwhile to offer—both the sound of my voice and my ideas.

YOU ARE NEVER TOO OLD TO ATTEMPT SOMETHING NEW AND EXCEL AT IT IF YOU PUT YOUR MIND TO IT.

Don't let age keep you from pursuing something that gives you a sense of purpose or enjoyment.

I was sixty years old when I learned to play golf. At age seventy, Donald Trump became the oldest U.S. President to assume the office.

WHEN YOUR HAND'S GOING FOR THE CLOCK AND YOUR FOOT'S GOING FOR THE FLOOR, YOU'LL NEVER BE LATE NO MORE.

Don't delay. Get up each day with a sense of purpose.

Now in my late seventies, I could sleep late and putter around the house, but that would bore me to death. I enjoy my life by getting up early and filling each day with meaningful pursuits. In many situations, I do more in one day than people half my age accomplish over a week.

Get it while it's hot. Take advantage of opportunities when they arise.
While you're waiting around, your competition is moving in.

In the early years of Metro Waterproofing, I'd stop whatever I was doing to pick up business. If I spotted potential, even if on vacation with my family, I'd stop to write up a proposal to get the job. We continue to pursue fantastic opportunities and win the best contracts with an attitude that we want and appreciate the business.

Don't let a tragedy turn you into a tragic person.
No one reaches adulthood without experiencing heartbreaks and disappointments.

I've suffered serious physical injuries from a fall and a car accident. Metro Waterproofing also had a devastating fire. Instead of giving up, I gave more of myself, received more, and gained more than I ever imagined.

Have a positive attitude.
It doesn't matter if you're working, fishing or making love, the good will be highlighted if that's your focus.

After falling off that scaffolding, I focused on the two loves of my life, Sandra and Theresa. My determination to live out my life and provide for them as a husband and father inspired and motivated me to get up and do what was necessary to heal my body.

IF YOU DO WHAT'S RIGHT, THEN YOUR LIFE WILL BE GOOD. Pay attention to that little bell that tells you right from wrong. It'll never let you down.

I loved my prized Corvette, but when it hit me that the car could buy a home for someone in need, selling the vehicle and donating the proceeds to Habitat for Humanity brought more joy to me than a pretty machine on wheels ever could have.

When you give everything, He returns the blessings to you—hundredfold. Remember that we are placed on this earth to love one another.

PRAISE FOR CLYDE STRICKLAND AND *WHAT CAN I DO?*

"By not asking what God and our country can do for us, but rather what we can and must do for our Creator and our nation, Clyde Strickland's 'lead by example' book is a must read!"
– Evangelist Alveda King, Alveda King Ministries

"Clyde truly came from nothing, walked the walk, took life head on, and believes in God and our Country! I'm proud to say Clyde is a great friend and inspiration to me, and all are blessed that know him. Clyde loves America with all his heart and wants to leave our country better for our children's futures. We need more Clydes."
– Mark Andol, President of General Welding & Fabricating, Inc. & Founder/Owner of the Made In America Store

"Clyde Strickland is one of the great modern-day disciples of Christ and a true American prayer warrior and patriot! With unwavering joy and energy, Clyde Strickland is prayerfully

and philanthropically taking action to bring healing our great nation!"
– Stewart Cink, PGA Tour, 2009 British Open Champion

"Clyde Strickland is one of the greatest American patriots. I only need four words to describe this great American: Faith, Family, Friends and Freedom."
– Ricky Lee, Country Music Artist

"Clyde Strickland is the proof of the American dream! His story reminds every boy and girl that you can succeed and make a difference. Read this book and see how you can be a better Christian, patriot, and business leader."
– Phil Waldrep, Phil Waldrep Ministries, Decatur, AL

"Clyde Strickland's story is a God-story. It is an amazing story of how the Lord can take an ordinary human being and use him for great things in this world. Clyde not only loves Jesus, he lives with Jesus, minute by minute and hour by hour. As a man of much abiding prayer, the Holy Spirit has empowered him to minister to the needs of everyday people in very practical ways. You will find this book deeply inspiring and encouraging!"
– The Most Rev'd Dr. Foley Beach, Archbishop and Primate, Anglican Church in North America Bishop, Anglican Diocese of the South

"The son of a North Carolina sharecropper, from his first job off the farm peeling potatoes, to his building, rebuilding and expanding one of the nation's largest and most

successful waterproofing companies, Clyde Strickland has been a dedicated learner, teacher, faithful Christian layman and philanthropist, candidly sharing with others the bedrock principles of success he learned along the way, often the hard way. Parents should give their children and grandchildren copies of *What Can I Do?* Making America great again will require more than adjustments to public policy. But young Americans—whatever their race, ethnicity, advantage or disadvantage—who learn the 'how-tos' of success that Clyde so vividly relates via his colorful, real-life stories, will do their part to make America great again!"
– Pierre Bynum, Chaplain & National Prayer Director, Family Research Council, Washington, DC

"Clyde Strickland is a remarkable person who continues to amaze me with his accomplishments. He has a great zest for life and is always upbeat and positive. A man of great faith, Clyde is extremely generous with his time, talent and treasure. I'm proud to call Clyde a great friend and admire the way he has lived his life."
– Phil Wolfe, President & CEO of Gwinnett Medical Center

"If someone were to ask me what it meant to be a mighty man of God, I would tell them the definition could be found in the dictionary under the name 'Clyde Strickland.' No man has defined what it means to be a servant leader better than Clyde. He is a patriotic American Veteran, a master storyteller, incredible spiritual mentor, encouraging optimist, dedicated and giving philanthropist, and the best example of a

Godly husband and father that a guy like me could ever hope to have speak into my life. My adventures with Clyde and his wife Sandra are what legends are made of, and I praise the Lord, He graced me with the enormous pleasure to know and learn from this mighty man of God."
– Nathaniel Thomas McGill, Producer & Director of *American Made Movie.*

"Clyde's inspirational story is a perfect illustration of how hard work and determination can allow someone to have an impact on their community and this country. He is a great American!"
– Vincent Vittorio, Founder and CEO of Life Is My Movie Entertainment

"Gwinnett County, Georgia, was one of the most populated counties in the United States without an open-heart surgery program for its citizens, that is until Clyde Strickland and others got involved. Through his generosity and diligent efforts, Gwinnett Medical Center built the Strickland Heart Center and opened the heart program in January 2012. There is no doubt that God led Clyde's passion in this opportunity for the community to have state-of-the-art surgical care close to home, and we are very thankful for his deep commitment and concern for others. Lives have been saved. To borrow one of Clyde's favorite quotes, 'Thank you, Jesus,' for Clyde Strickland."
– David A. Langford, M.D., Chief of Cardiovascular Surgery, Strickland Heart Center

"Clyde Strickland knows that success—for an individual, a family, a community, a nation—does not happen by accident. It takes committed citizens who are willing to be engaged and to be leaders. This timely book is a call to action for every individual to get involved in building the America of the future."
– Daniel Kaufman, Brigadier General, U.S. Army (Retired)

96759245R00124

Made in the USA
Columbia, SC
01 June 2018